Maria Antonietta Crippa

ANTONI GAUDÍ
1852–1926

From Nature to Architecture

TASCHEN

KÖLN LONDON LOS ANGELES MADRID PARIS TOKYO

Illustration page ► Antoní Gaudi as a young man
Illustration page 2 ► Gaudí's sketches of the
hexagonal tiles which were used for the pavement
outside the Casa Milà and as floor-covering in
some rooms

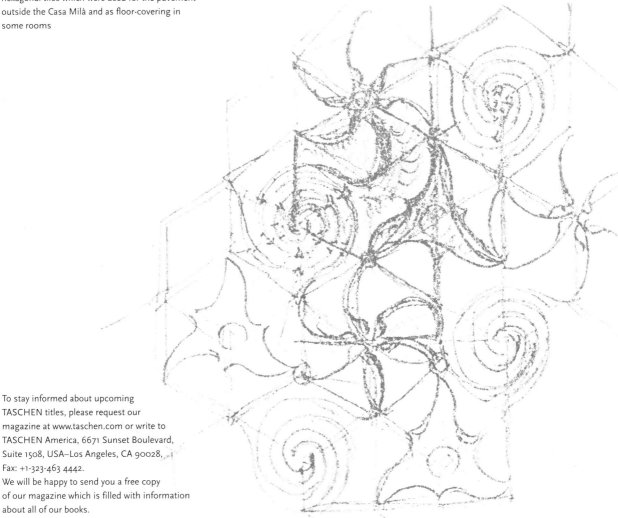

To stay informed about upcoming
TASCHEN titles, please request our
magazine at www.taschen.com or write to
TASCHEN America, 6671 Sunset Boulevard,
Suite 1508, USA–Los Angeles, CA 90028,
Fax: +1-323-463 4442.
We will be happy to send you a free copy
of our magazine which is filled with information
about all of our books.

Edited by ► Peter Gössel, Bremen
Project manager ► Swantje Schmidt, Bremen
Design and layout ► Gössel und Partner, Bremen
Text edited by ► Susanne Klinkhamels, Chrisitane
Blass, Cologne
Translation ► Jeremy Carden, Florence

Printed in Germany
ISBN 3-8228-2518-2

Contents

Introduction

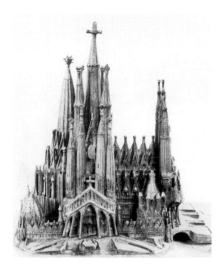

Final version of the plaster model of the Sagrada Família, restored by recomposing fragments not destroyed in 1936

When Antoni Gaudí was born in 1852, in Reus, near Barcelona, Catalonia was going through a phase of social change. The industrial revolution was modifying not only traditional social structures but also the whole concept of urban planning. In fact, the changes in industrial production methods engineered by the middle classes led to a rapid growth of the cities, the need for new types of buildings, especially residential and commercial ones, the invention of the train and steam-powered ship, and a general abandonment of the traditional world of agriculture. This process started later in Catalonia than in other areas of Western Europe and the US, but much earlier than the rest of the Iberian peninsula. The framework of the region's rural culture, especially the cohesion of the family structure, remained intact for a long time, but there was a rapid development of a set of dynamic relations in marked contrast to the bureaucratic slowness of the nation's capital, Madrid, still a city of modest dimensions.

In 1851, the year before Gaudí was born, London hosted the first Great Exhibition of the best industrial products in the world. It was held in a purpose-built, prefabricated, transparent structure that resembled a greenhouse, hence its name, Crystal Palace. On display inside this glass and cast-iron structure, brilliantly designed by Joseph Paxton, were the most modern technologies and the finest craft products from round the world, including the colonies.

However, it was evident that the technological and the craft worlds existed in an unstable balance that tended to be at the expense of the latter, because there was enormous and increasing enthusiasm for mass production and machines of everyday use. Not everyone, however, was in favour of this progress and the results it brought, and there was a good deal of bitter resistance, in the name of art and of the wealth of humanity and technical skills which traditional craft production had protected and nurtured for centuries.

In this period of innovation and of enthusiastic but not always reasonable use of new production methods, lifestyles that had existed for centuries crumbled all too rapidly. However, in the middle of the 19th century, innovators and traditionalists clashed head-on in all fields, sometimes violently and with bitter polemic tones. At the same time, many rural peasants and craftspeople became industrial workers, usually very poor ones, and they no longer possessed personal and irreplaceable skills. Even their cultural forms and their religious and civic conscience were hard hit. Traditional society – hermetic, socially stable and primarily rural – was about to be substituted by a dynamic, open and progressive society.

Artists were also influenced by the social and cultural turbulence brought about by these transformations. By the end of the 19th century, the stage was already set for the avant-garde movements that would lead to an upheaval in traditional figuration, themes and techniques. This process was aided by the invention of photography and film – new media for a new world –, which were reproducible and capable of communicating in an immediately effective way with large numbers of people. The first heated outburst of the artistic crisis that was underway occurred in Paris in 1855, during the

Facing page:
Interior of Gaudí's workshop on the Sagrada Família site, with different-sized scale models of parts of the church

second Exposition Universelle. There was a rift between the artists, and they decided to show their paintings in two separate halls, a reflection of two basically different attitudes. Jean-Auguste-Dominique Ingres showed in the official hall, Eugène Delacroix and Théodore Rousseau in a Salon des Réfusés, the hall of those who felt rejected by the academic authorities. Just a few years later, in 1861, Edouard Manet scandalized the art world with his famous painting, *Déjeuner sur l'herbe*. It is no accident that these painters' rejection of preestablished aesthetic canons and their insubordination towards the powers that be, in favour of greater subjective sincerity, were accompanied by a desire on the part of other groups of artists and architects to recover traditional working practices and religious sentiment. The exemplary model for this was the human quality of the craft world and medieval design energy. In the world of painting, communities of artists sprang up, like the Pre-Raphaelite Brotherhood founded by Dante Gabriel Rossetti and other artists. In architecture, attention focused on conserving or restoring medieval cathedrals, together with a marked moralization of the rationale of new projects, which at the time were generally eclectic in style.

Water-colour design by the student Gaudí for a large university entrance hall, 22 october 1877

In *The Seven Lamps of Architecture*, published in 1849, the English critic John Ruskin invited his contemporaries to resist the social, human and aesthetic decay stemming from massive and extremely rapid urban migration from rural areas. 1854 saw the publication of the *Dictionnaire raisonné de l'architecture française du XIe au XVIe siècle* by the architect and historian of French architecture, Eugène-Emmanuel Viollet-le-Duc. This encyclopaedic work conveyed the author's deep fascination with the bold experimental rationality of cathedral builders. Viollet-le-Duc analysed the structural characteristics and architectural framework of these enormous buildings; he examined modifications over time and made suggestions about how to conserve them and also ways of completing them in the same style. He gave readers an insight into the taste of medieval builders, with an in-depth study of principles of construction, the properties of materials and the static behaviour of structures, thereby involving readers in the logic of an artistic and constructive system that was open to further developments in the 19th century. In other works, Viollet-le-Duc also proposed the use of new materials, above all cast iron, in modern buildings like schools and public halls. These obeyed the same conceptual building logic he had noted in the cathedrals.

The work of Ruskin and Viollet-le-Duc quickly circulated in Europe and America, becoming a source of guidance for the young architects and builders then being called upon to produce solutions to new housing and urban needs.

In the uproar of violent political clashes at a national level, there was growing interest in Catalonia in emphasizing the cultural specificity of the Catalan identity, accompanied by the pursuit of political and regional autonomy from Madrid. This was effectively promoted by a number of leading figures from various fields of society – politicians, entrepreneurs, intellectuals and members of Catholic ecclesiastical institutions. For young professionals, this represented an excellent opportunity for work and social promotion, and, invited to celebrate history and enrich contemporary culture, they contributed to creating a sense of cultural belonging.

Barcelona was already caught up in the industrial development, social transformation and cultural and artistic debate briefly outlined above when, in 1869, a young Antoni Gaudí accompanied his brother Francesc to Barcelona, where the latter had decided to study medicine. In September of that year, Spain was thrown into turmoil by major socialist and republican revolts, which ended with the collapse of the kingdom of Queen Isabella II. The two brothers were soon joined by their father, who looked after them and sold some family land to help fund their studies. The three of them were from the nearby town of Reus, which was not without a certain cultural vitality of its own. Like his parents and his wife's family, Gaudí's father was a copper-smith. Antoni had often spent time in the family workshop during his childhood and adolescence, admiring the solid volumes of pans and the delicate forms of alembics. He was greatly struck by the spatial working of these objects, and this shaped an uncommon ability to perceive and mentally represent three-dimensional volumes and structures. His thoughtful, reflective temperament, accentuated by the early onset of rheumatic illnesses, also made him a keen observer of nature and the forms of trees, flowers and animals. Finally, during his early studies he also developed an interest in drawing and architecture.

In order to gain admittance to the Provincial School of Architecture, which was founded in 1870 and became an official university faculty in 1875, he enrolled in preparatory courses at the Faculty of Sciences. In 1873, the year he became an architectural student, the First Republic was proclaimed in Madrid; this soon came to an end, in 1874, following a coup d'état by General Pavía which restored the monarchy. The young student observed what was happening also through the positions assumed by his university professors. In 1878, the first ten Catalan architects graduated from the School of Architecture, followed, the next year, by another four, one of whom was Antoni Gaudí. The city walls had been demolished in 1854 and in 1859 Barcelona was subject to a new urbanization plan, called Eixample, drawn up by the engineer Ildefons Cerdà. Initiated in 1860, it pursued principles of rationality, equity and modern efficiency for the growth of the city, without defining any boundaries. It envisaged a grid pattern of urbanization and was based on studies of demographic trends, traffic and the regulation of primary and secondary services.

Young architects were taught a range of disciplines – technical, scientific, artistic, historical, archaeological – in order to create a new professional figure quite distinct from the *maestros de obras*, building site experts, or the academic architects working in fine art schools. They were asked to contribute in a concrete fashion to the reawakening of the Catalan identity, to restore churches, convents and old palaces, and to embellish the rapidly expanding city with imposing public buildings possessing a solemn, representative monumentality. Gaudí's student designs reflect this; there are studies for a landing jetty; a monumental fountain for Plaça de Catalunya; an assembly hall for the university.

In these formative years, Gaudí was caught up by a widespread interest for Paris in refined circles. The Catalan capital admired Paris' consolidated artistic pre-eminence over the rest of Europe and the Western world, besides its strong propensity for rationality. However, the citizens of Barcelona were also open to influences from across the Atlantic. The Spanish crown had allowed them to emigrate to the Americas only from the end of the 18th century onwards, but the exodus towards the colonies had then been extensive, the preferred destination being Cuba. Some of them later returned with their newly acquired wealth and the vitality they had assimilated from the Cubans. They have "Paris as a conscious ideal and La Havana as an unconscious model", wrote Eduardo Mendoza.

The complex modernization of Barcelona was thus influenced by two different models, which imbued its leading protagonists with dynamism, a joyful openness to

Cast-iron, six-lantern street lamp for Plaça Reial in Barcelona, based on a design by Gaudí (1878–79)

life, an interest in art and a sense that they were culturally different from Madrid. In the second half of the 19th century, this mix of two cultures produced entrepreneurs who monopolized a number of national markets – dynamic, cultured figures who were sometimes animated by a spirit of generous patronage. The most important of these was Eusebi Güell i Bacigalupi, who met Barcelona's most brilliant architect when Gaudí was just starting out on his career. When the 1888 Exposición Universal projected Barcelona onto the world scene, Güell and Gaudí shared the same political and social ideals.

1888 saw the inauguration of Gaudí's first building in the heart of the ancient city centre, Palau Güell. By this time he was well-established and in great demand by the upper- middle classes. And since he had been directing work on the Sagrada Família since 1883, he also came into contact with the most prominent ecclesiastical figures in Spain. If at the beginning of his career, his modest origins and his sense of social justice had led him to gravitate towards workers' cooperatives, his involvement with Eusebi Güell subsequently took him along a path closely bound up, in personal and professional terms, with the affirmation of Catalan identity, both its traditions and its modernity.

Little is known about his personal life, and it seems that he was almost entirely absorbed by his work as an architect. The only notable episode was a moment of religious crisis, or perhaps maturation, when in 1893, at the age of forty-one, he adopted such a radical Lent fast that he put his life seriously at risk.

As soon as he completed his studies, Gaudí opened a studio in Plaça de Sant Jaume in Barcelona. His first important commission came in 1878 from a textile manufacturing cooperative called La Obrera Mataronense, the first worker-owned factory in Spain. Also important, because it drew the attention of the city bourgeoisie, was his 1879 design for the refurbishment of a pharmacy in Passeig de Gràcia for Joan Gibert i Saler, a relative of the Güell family. A skilled draughtsman, Gaudí was also called upon to decorate the interiors of churches and convent chapels. For the same reason he soon began to be consulted by public bodies as well; in 1880, together with his friend, the engineer José Sarramalera, he designed monumental street-lamps for the promenade along the sea wall in Barcelona.

As he did not yet have any major projects, he also worked as assistant to one of his former professors, Joan Martorell i Montells. In 1882, he designed for him in a neo-Gothic style the church of the monastery of the Holy Spirit in Cuevas de Almanzora (Almería), and another two churches, one for the Salesians and the other for the Jesuits in Barcelona. He also produced a neo-Gothic design, never executed, for the façade of Barcelona Cathedral. In the same year he received the important commission to design a hunting lodge in El Garraf on the Mediterranean coast for Count Eusebi Güell, who had immediately recognized his talent after seeing a showcase of leather products at the Exposition Universelle in Paris in 1878.

In 1883, just five years after graduating, Gaudí could boast three important commissions, which projected him into the circle of the leading Catalan architects. That year he started work on two exclusive residential sites, Casa Vicens in Barcelona and Villa El Capricho in Comillas (Santander), and he was appointed chief architect of the Sagrada Família. Work on this had just started, the foundation stone having been laid the previous year. It was an expiatory temple undertaken at the wishes of the Associació Espiritual de Devots de Sant Josep, which had been founded to sustain Catholic

Gaudí illustrating the work underway on the Sagrada Família to the papal nuncio, Mons. Ragonesi, and the Bishop of Barcelona, Mons. Roig, 1915

social theories amongst the Catalan working classes after St Joseph had been proclaimed patron of the Catholic Church in 1869–70 during Vatican I. The initiative had been supported by the publisher Josep Maria Bocabella, who had bought a vast plot of land on the outskirts of the city and established a committee (the Junta Constructora del Temple) to oversee its realization.

The architect Francesc de Paula Villar i Lozano, Director of the Provincial School of Architecture and a member of the Academy of Fine Arts, offered his ambitious neo-Gothic design free of charge. Following strong disagreement between Villar and Martorell, who was a member of the Junta, Villar resigned, upon which Martorell recommended his young 31-year-old assistant. Gaudí was appointed on 3 November 1883, and soon after, in April 1884, he signed his first project document. The wishes of the promoters – respected through to the present day – was that the building should be funded entirely from donations made to the Associació Espiritual de Devots de Sant Josep. As these were initially rather limited, Gaudí had to carry out the early work following Villar's plans. In the meantime, Eusebi Güell gave him his first important commission in 1883, the reorganization of Finca Güell, which now houses the Reial Càtedra de Gaudí. This is famous above all for its wrought-iron dragon gate, a metaphor of the garden of the Hesperides, celebrated in the epic poem *L'Atlàntida* by the Catalan priest Jacint Verdaguer.

None of Gaudí's work mentioned thus far lay within the city boundaries of the time. Nor did his next few works, which included the Col·legi de les Teresianes, the completion of a building that had already in part been constructed and which was commissioned in 1889 by the founder of the Compañía Santa Teresa de Jesús, Father Enric d'Ossó i Cervelló. The building was in the nearby municipality of Sant Gervasi. Two other works from the same period were also outside Barcelona: the Palacio Episcopal at Astorga, which he directed between 1889 and 1893, and the Casa Fernández y Andrés or Casa de los Botines (1891–94), in Léon.

The first disagreements between enthusiastic supporters and irate denigrators of Gaudí's work emerged between 1888 and 1890, upon completion of Palau Güell in the heart of the old city centre. At the Exposición Universal held in Barcelona in 1888, architects belonging to the la Renaixença movement contributed to the realization of the exhibition pavilions and showed their architectural designs. The Director of Works was Professor Elies Rogent, head of the city's School of Architecture. The mayor commissioned Gaudí to decorate the Saló de Cent and the steps of honour of the municipal building. The project never got off the ground, but he exhibited his architectural designs in the artistic section and designed a pavilion in the maritime section, commissioned by the Marqués de Comillas for the Compañía Transatlántica.

1888 marked the moment of transition from his expressive, mainly eclectic phase to a more freely modernist one, the moment in which his original contribution to Catalan Modernisme first began to blossom. This was a variant of a movement that was active in the last decades of the 19th and the beginning of the 20th century; substantially similar throughout the West, it took a number of regionally-differentiated forms such as Art Nouveau, Jugendstil, Floreale, Sezession and Liberty.

Catalan Modernisme, which celebrated the aspirations of the upper and middle classes, its view of a purposeful life and the representative nature of public spaces, was expressed in monumental public and private architecture and exuberant forms and colours. It promoted the craft work of ceramicists, blacksmiths and ebony workers,

Wrought-iron lectern made by Gaudí for the Sagrada Família

mixing various historicist influences and assimilating innovations in technology and construction. Leading architects in the movement included Enric Sagnier (1858–1931); Josep Domènech i Estapà (1858–1917); Pere Falqués i Urpí (1850–1916); Bonaventura Bassegoda i Amigó (1862–1940); Cèsar Martinell i Brunet (1888–1973); Josep Maria Jujol (1879–1949) and many others.

Gaudí distinguished himself through his attention to nature and the importance he attributed to geometric forms. These differences led him to greater introspection; he cultivated only his deepest friendships and he gradually moved away from the high-society circles that had attracted him as a young man. Between 1890 and 1914 he produced the buildings and gardens which scholars universally consider to be his masterpieces: Casa Calvet (1898–1900), still vaguely neo-Baroque; the gaily-coloured Casa Batlló (1904–06) and the plastic, monolithic Casa Milà (1906–10) on Passeig de Gràcia in Barcelona; Villa Bellesguard (1900–05) in an historically important outlying area of the city; Park Güell (1900–14), a highly singular city-garden which soon became a public park; the remodelling of the cathedral of Palma de Mallorca (1903–14); the crypt of the church in the workers' village, or Colònia Güell (1898–1915), at Santa Coloma de Cervelló; the classrooms (1909) of the Sagrada Família.

In this work, and also on the Sagrada Família site, his brand of Modernisme soon evolved into an original organicism which had no parallels in contemporary Western culture. This organic-naturalistic orientation imbued the form and structure of his buildings and drew on the expressive possibilities of traditional Catalan construction techniques. These also offered Gaudí an opportunity to explore geometric forms previously unused in architecture but widely present in nature. He always designed from three-dimensional models made from plaster, wood, wires and counterweights, with cloth to simulate the surfaces. The model was the principal instrument in the development of his ideas; drawing was also important to him, but as he said to his students, he conceived forms directly in space.

Throughout his long professional life, he also explored, with great originality, two paths of research. First of all, he gradually deepened his knowledge of geometry. As a young man, he spent time in the university library consulting engineering and architectural treatises that described the mechanical advantages of the continuous catenary curve, which until that time had been used only by engineers in designing suspension bridges. Overcoming aesthetic objections, he used it in various ways together with the ellipse and the hyperbola. To realize the profile of this curve, the pillars of his final works were inclined.

He soon moved on from plane to spatial geometric forms; he subjected architectural form to a configuration of spatial surfaces formed only by straight lines, known to mathematicians as ruled surfaces. After his first attempts, his work became increasingly complex in form, also because he found ways to realize projects using uncomplicated and inexpensive traditional building methods and materials, above all bricks and mortar. Amongst the traditional techniques, the one he rendered most celebrated was the bóveda tabicada, a vault covering made using overlapping layers of small, highly resistant tiles held in place by lime mortar.

His role as director of the large Sagrada Família site stimulated him to rethink all the aspects of the artistic and technological culture he had accumulated and to put them at the service of the architectural theme of the church. He soon developed a disinterested dedication to his task. During an economic crisis which forced him to

Porter's lodge in the Park Güell

suspend work in 1914 he even went so far as to personally seek contributions to fund the work. In the last few years of his life, he declined all other professional projects and led a sober, secluded lifestyle. His aim was to prepare – in the form of plaster models and drawings – a rational continuation of the church, which he predicted could be completed in about two hundred years.

He spent all his time on site, except for Sunday mornings, when he would walk along the seafront with a group of young architects, who questioned him and faithfully wrote down everything he had to say about his relationship with nature, the Mediterranean Sea, the political and social reality of Catalonia, art and his architectural works. These notes were later transcribed and carefully classified.

Gaudí died on 10 June 1926 at the age of seventy-four, three days after being knocked down by a tram. His funeral was attended by an immense crowd of Catalans, who were aware that they were bidding a final farewell to their greatest architect.

Gaudí succeeded in drawing on profound, ecological meanings in architecture. He was simultaneously a traditionalist and an innovator. He managed to imbue his architecture with a systematic and enduring bond between static structure and architectural form, between spatial form and decoration. His contribution encompasses the architecture of the individual building and that of the landscape. In his work, there is also a pervasive sense of an intensely carnal sacrality which has activated a symbolic and communicative dimension.

Gaudí's workshop on the Sagrada Família site in 1926

1883 – 1885 · El Capricho
Comillas (Santander)

Ground-floor plan of the villa
There are three short flights of steps under the entrance portico, positioned diagonally in relation to the general longitudinal development of the wall.

Gaudí was asked by Máximo Díaz de Quijano, the brother-in-law of Eusebi Güell and subsequently nominated Marqués de Comillas by the King of Spain, to design a holiday residence on the coast at Comillas in the province of Santander. The building was named El Capricho because of its original appearance. It is located in the heart of a chestnut wood on the slopes of a hill. In building it, Gaudí took account of the slope of the land, which faced north towards a green valley running down towards the sea. He organized the building with a prevalently horizontal arrangement, orientating it so the day areas looked onto the valley and installing double glazing.

Part of the building sits on a plane obtained by excavating a stretch of land, which is contained by a tall, solid wall that also acts as a sitting-out area in the garden behind the house. The exterior walls of the compact villa are decorated with horizontal bands of motifs. The main façade on the ground floor is accentuated by protruding rusticated stone that is greyish yellow-ochre in colour. On the first floor of the main façade and throughout the others, the wall consists of an alternating sequence of high-background iridescent brickwork and rows of majolica tiles, most of which were decorated either with a relief pattern of a sunflower or its leaves.

The distributional logic of the interior rooms is similar to that of Casa Vicens: the kitchens and utility rooms are in the basement, while the first floor has the large reception rooms and a smoking room covered with small Arab-style plaster vaults. The lower sections of the walls are faced with painted ceramic tiles, the upper parts with papier mâché. Built to house many guests, the villa has a series of bedrooms with independent bathrooms, linked, via a connecting room, to a double-height living room which is the focus of the house.

The construction work was not directed by Gaudí personally, but by the architect Cristóbal Cascante i Colom (1857–1889), with whom he had studied at university, according to a highly-detailed model Gaudí prepared for him.

Details of the wooden coffering, with bronze boss and escutcheon ornamentation

Facing page:
View of the villa in the chestnut wood
In the foreground, the entrance portico with the tall viewing tower.

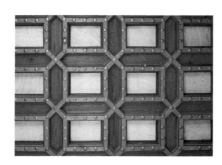

1883 – 1887 · Finca Güell

Avinguda de Pedralbes, 7, Barcelona

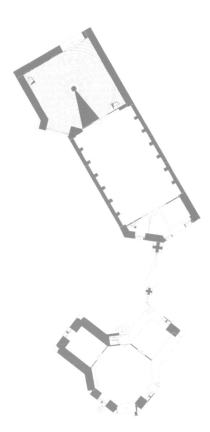

Ground-floor plans of the two Finca Güell buildings: the lodge, a three-block L-shaped structure, and the stables and riding ring

Facing page:
Finca Güell building facing onto Avinguda de Pedralbes

Eusebi Güell inherited from his father vast tracts of farm land in a hill zone on the outskirts of Barcelona called Les Corts de Sarrià. Here the architect Joan Martorell i Montells had already built an extensive Caribbean-style house reminiscent of Cuba and the Dominican Republic, where the Güell family had grown rich before returning to their native country. Eusebi Güell bought more land around this already vast property, then commissioned Gaudí in 1883 to reorganize what until then had been a French-style park and to build some new constructions – a lodge and a stable complex. In the reorganized Romantic-style park, Gaudí introduced many Mediterranean plants – pines, eucalyptuses, magnolias, cypresses, palms –, two fountains and a pergola. Most of the park and the Caribbean house were subsequently sold by Eusebi's son to the Royal Crown of Spain, who transformed it into a Barcelona residence and named it Palau de Pedralbes, now the prestigious home of the Municipal Museum of Ceramics. The actual Finca Güell consists of a garden, with one of the two fountains, and the pergola, where a catenary arch can be seen.

In front of the garden, on the perimeter of the land marked by the road, there are two buildings known as the Pavellons de la Finca Güell – a lodge and a stable complex – which are linked by a double entrance for pedestrians and, formerly, carriages. The property is still surrounded by the original wall (with secondary openings), which runs along Avinguda de Pedralbes and Carrer George R. Collins.

On the left-hand side, looking in from outside, is the lodge house, which consists of three sections. The central one has a polygonal base and houses a large living room covered by a hyperbola-section dome built according to the Catalan method. The central unit is flanked by two more modestly sized cubes; on the ground floor are rooms covered by small beamed vaults, while on the first floor there are bedrooms with hyperbola-section vaulting. This kind of section permitted the insertion of ventilation shafts at the top, faced on the outside with coloured ceramic tiles.

The lodge thus has an L-shaped plan with two equal-sized wings. At the junctions between the three units are the entrance and stair areas. It is very interesting how Gaudí interwove static structural components and a variety of surface decoration. He used raw earth, a low-cost material with good insulating properties, for the buffer wall. Baked clay bricks in iridescent colours ranging from red to yellow were positioned in the corners and in the sections of the wall most subject to compression forces. These were left in full view and bound together with layers of mortar containing fragments of coloured glass. The raw earth surfaces were covered by prefabricated concrete blocks with clear semi-circular undulations and relief spherules. The coping on the outside walls is faced with normal, dark-red, baked clay bricks arranged in a lively castellated pattern (on a horizontal plane jutting out from the wall) with a gradually overhanging vertical profile. By using these techniques, Gaudí was able to obtain, using cheap materials, a well-insulated sealing surface that explicitly recalled Mudéjar art. He also achieved intensely vibrant polychrome effects in the light. On the right-hand side, looking in from outside, are the stables, also on the edge of the road; they are preceded by the entrance and service rooms and completed by a square-plan riding area covered by a lantern-topped dome. Like the lodge, this second building also has mixed walling, erected by skilled workers brought in especially from the province of Lleida. The stables, which now house the library of the Reial Càtedra de Gaudí, has a rectangular plan and a rhythmic sequence of transverse arches. These are linked by small parabolic-section vaults permitting the insertion of large windows along the two long façades.

Finca Güell is known above all for its extraordinary wrought-iron entrance gate. There is a double entrance. Pedestrians enter through a gate with a parabolic arch profile; the same form is repeated in the pattern on the adjoining brick wall, which rests on a high stone base. Here Gaudí created a sculptural masterpiece in wrought iron, his favourite material. He built it, like the majority of his ironwork designs, in the workshop of the blacksmith Joan Oñós. The dragon and golden apple tree on top of the pillar from which the gate hangs makes the Pavellons de la Finca Güell a suggestive architectural metaphor of a Greek myth – the final labour of Hercules, who stole the golden apples from the garden of the Hesperides. The myth was narrated by the priest and poet Jacint Verdaguer, a friend of Güell and Gaudí, in his epic poem *L'Atlàntida*, dedicated to the Marqués de Comillas, for whom he acted as a spiritual guide. In the poem he celebrated the mythical origins and magnificent destiny of the Catalan people.

The outer wall of the porter's lodge
Whilst the windows with their catenary arches are set back into the brick outer wall, the masonry itself consists of compressed clay, faced with semi-circular concrete moulds.

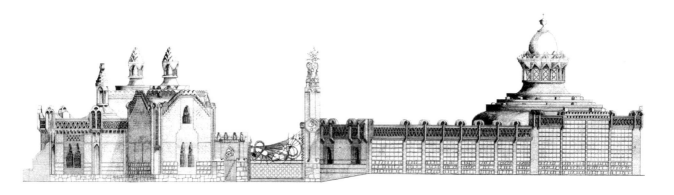

Drawing of the elevation along Avinguda de Pedralbes
In the centre, the wrought-iron gate with the dragon figure, hung on a high pillar that is topped by the tree of golden apples, also in wrought iron.

Wrought-iron carriage gateway
The lower register consists of a square mesh made from twisted bars with the holes on the diagonal, filled by solid, wrought iron squares. In the upper register is the open-jawed dragon with bat's wings.

1883–1888 · Casa Vicens
Carrer de Les Carolines, 18–24, Barcelona

Ground-floor plan of the house

The first bourgeois home Gaudí designed was Casa Vicens, which overlooked a narrow street that was later widened and is now called Carrer de Les Carolines; situated in the Gràcia neighbourhood, it was subsequently swallowed up within the administrative boundaries of the city. The project was commissioned by the stockbroker Manuel Vicens i Montaner. The building is still well conserved and was enlarged in 1925–1927 by a student of Gaudí, the architect Joan Baptista Serra de Martínez, who consulted closely with his elderly master before intervening on the building and garden. From Gaudí himself we know that the many floral and plant motifs adorning the building were inspired by plant life he found on the site: "When I went to take the measurements, the ground was totally covered with the little yellow flowers that I used as the ornamental theme in the ceramics. I also found a lush palm, and palmettes, fused in metal, cover the grid of the gate and the door to the house."

Here, as in his other secluded bourgeois homes with gardens, he gave form to the youthful idea of the domestic home as a small nation offering a protective environment for its members. In fact, Casa Vicens was intended to provide its occupants with well-being, hygiene, beauty and a close relationship with nature. Gaudí also began his life-long exploration of how to achieve the best possible ventilation and lighting inside the building, using carefully chosen filters – which he often invented himself – between the interior and the exterior.

The vast residence is a detached, three-storey block with undulating polychromatic façades. In the basement there is the kitchen and the utility rooms The ground floor includes the entrance hall; a large, heavily decorated dining room opening onto a south-facing veranda; a smoking corner covered by Muslim-style motifs, muqarnas, forming a false dome, closed in by windows etched with a leafy palm pattern. On the top floor there are two bedrooms with plaster walls and fresco decorations inspired by vegetation found on the banks of the nearby river Cassoles.

The building has a simple load-bearing wall structure with wooden beam floors. The skeleton of the building is designed as to rigorously support the interior and exterior spatial articulation, and is completed by Mudéjar stylistic and ornamental variations.

Gaudí designed all the details with great care, personally deciding on all the furnishings and fittings, from the furniture to the sliding doors concealed within the walls and the ingenious locks on the cupboards, made of fused, gilded brass. The furnishings of the large dining room are also designed as to define the space architecturally, producing a varied and unbroken articulation between corner and wall furniture. The ceiling is decorated with polychrome papier mâché in the gaps between the wooden beams, with fruit and strawberry-tree flower motifs. The walls have climbing ivy graffitto designs.

The whole exterior skin of the building makes extensive use of wall divisions and projecting brick brackets which draw on an Islamic building technique. The corner tower by the road is very elaborate with increasingly overhanging projections. The projections and overhangs are always accompanied by a complex polychromy of bricks, rubble and checkered and floral ceramic tiles. The forms and the gaps between floors accentuate a chiaroscuro effect that reaches its maximum expression in the upper part of the building. At the top of the façades there is also a gallery, once closed in by oriental-design wooden latticework. There is a walkway all the way round the edge of the roof, with seats out in the open and beneath the corner towers.

The property is surrounded by a rubble wall topped by a wrought-iron strip with a broad, dwarf-palm foliate pattern on a rigid support. The foliate pattern was obtained using a terracotta cast. Gaudí surrounded the building with three gardens; a small one separates the house from the road, a second one is laid out in front of the main living area of the house and consists of round beds of palms; in a third one, to one side, there are fruit trees.

Interior of the dining room, with a band of furniture running round the edge

Fireplace in the dining room

Detail of the module of the wrought-iron gate, with a dwarf palm-leaf ornamental motif

Above:
Original furnishings in the living room

Left:
Garden of the house after 1925
In the foreground, a round chapel, behind it the
rectangle protecting the cascade. Both have been
destroyed.

1886–1890 · Palau Güell

Carrer Nou de la Rambla, 3–5, Barcelona

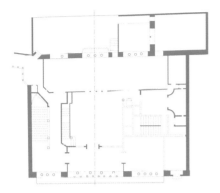

Plan of the main floor of the palace
The music room is in the middle. The drawing was exhibited at the 1910 Paris Exposition organized by the Société des Beaux-Arts.

This was the first building constructed by Gaudí for Eusebi Güell that was not in an outlying district but in the heart of Barcelona itself. The project took shape during what was a very lively period for the city, which celebrated its modernity – not only technological but in all fields – in 1888 with the Exposición Universal. In this climate, Güell, who was by now a friend of the architect, felt the need for a residence which adequately represented his social status and cultural ambitions. Historians note that Palau Güell was extremely expensive, that it was disliked by Güell's wife, a mother of ten, because it was too big, and that Eusebi himself did not live there for long; however, it was here that he grouped together his art collection and various items of cultural interest he had collected over the years on his travels. The plot of land, inherited from his father, which Güell designated for the building, is hemmed in between rather ordinary buildings, but is linked to another Güell property via a courtyard. The project required a great deal of Gaudí's time, and he came up with as many as twenty-five different solutions for the main façade.

Building work continued until 1890, but it was officially inaugurated in 1888 – the date is carved into the façade –, the year of the Exposición Universal. It immediately aroused fierce debate, reported in great detail by the local press. It was variously declared to be beautiful, Babylonic, more of a temple than a home, rare and precious, a wild luxury.

The street façade of the very tall ground floor is dominated by two imposing and markedly splayed parabolic arches, with solid-looking wrought-iron entrance gates worked into a mesh pattern. The gates were framed at the top by fixed elements, with the iron bent into soft undulations around the heraldic shields, which bear the initials of the owner. As a celebration of Catalan pride, in the space between the two stone arches there is a large cylindrical shield from which a small eagle is set to take off. The interweaving of strips, meshes and ribbons of iron decoration with plant and animal motifs render this Catalan crest a celebrated wrought-iron masterpiece. The rear of the building is equally detailed and sober, dominated by a substantial, overhanging veranda, where space was found for a bench. A wooden screen with adjustable shuttering sheltered it from the exterior.

The underground floor houses extensive stables accessible via a helicoidal ramp broken by substantial brick pillars with a diameter of up to 1.4 metres, which expand at the top into cone and pyramid frustums before joining the covering vaults.

The heart of the building is a vast apartment space, acoustically and visually protected from the exterior and rich in decorative detail, with tricks of perspective, scenographic effects and an interplay of vaguely neo-Gothic and Mudéjar motifs and modernist leanings. The centre of the apartment is a large room rising all the way to the roof, through which natural light filters in suggestively from outside. Pendentives rise from the four edges of the base cube; these permit the insertion of four parabolic-profile arches corresponding to the sides of the square and also provide support for a large parabolic dome. This has small openings in it, faced with hexagonal brown ala-

Facing page:
View from the gallery on the first floor to the music room below
The large door conceals a small recess in which there is a chapel with an altar.

Left:
The façade of the Palau Güell with adjacent buildings
Above the high ground floor rises the main storey with the rostrum. The façade is crowned by a fringe of merlons, and on the terrace-roof there are chimneys and a pinnacle.

baster tiles, and a large opening in the middle, on which there is a lantern spire which admits light from the outside and directs it into the room. During the day the visual effect of this vault is that of a kind of starry sky, and this can also be achieved at night thanks to appropriately positioned lamps near the openings.

The skill reflected in the technical, static-structural, ventilation, acoustic insulation and lighting solutions is as incredible as the display of craft ability in the finishing of all the details. This reaches its culmination on the roof terrace, which, as always with Gaudí, is usable. The twenty ventilation chimneys on the building and the cone of the towering lantern spire have been transformed into amazing colourful sculptures, loosely interlacing geometric solids faced with trencadís ceramics or left in bare stone or terracotta.

Facing page:
View from below the vault with catenary-curve section covering the music room
Light filters in from the top through holes in the vault and from high side windows.

26

Detail of the elevation facing the interior courtyard
A veranda of superimposed floors is shielded by wooden, adjustable grilles.

Immediately hailed as a marvel by local citizens, reported on in numerous English and American magazines, it was considered by many to be the symbol of the Catalan Renaixença movement, the architectural symbol of a culturally ambitious bourgeoisie committed to promoting the Catalan language and to generously supporting its artists.

Palau Güell is also the only work to have been completely finished by Gaudí which has come down to us intact. In 1984, it was declared a world heritage site by UNESCO.

Facing page:
Main reception room of the palace, with the interior colonnade of the gallery facing onto Carrer Nou de la Rambla

1889 – 1890 · Col·legi de les Teresianes

Carrer Granduxer, 85, Barcelona

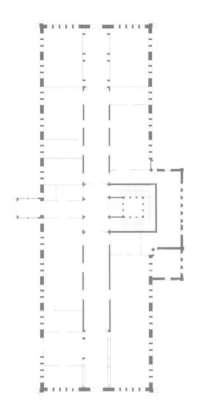

Plan of the college, which has a longitudinal layout

The entrance portico unit protrudes in the centre, while on the opposite side there is the stairwell. The central section is occupied by rows of corridors that are covered by fascinating catenary-curve arches and look onto interior wells of light.

Facing page:

Central ground floor corridor with brick, load-bearing brackets

A masonry catenary arch is in the centre.

Building was already under way in 1889 when Enric d'Ossó i Cervelló, the priest who had established the new female order of the Compañía de Santa Teresa de Jesús, asked Gaudí to complete it in a more imaginative way. The initial plan was for more than one building in what was then an outlying district of Barcelona but only the school and the nuns' residential quarters were eventually built. Furthermore, a lack of money prevented Gaudí from fully completing even this single building; the internal chapel (inaccessible from the road), in particular, was not his but was built at a later date.

The building is a compact rectangle that looks like an austere castle from the outside. The rhythm created by the four floors above ground, which become progressively less high, can be seen in the walls, and the building is topped with sharply-pointed, triangular battlements. Jutting out from the centre of the building at the front is a square unit that houses an entrance portico on the ground floor and a veranda on the two upper floors. At the back of the building, symmetrically opposite the main entrance, there is a larger protrusion with a secondary entrance and staircase.

The whole building was constructed using simple materials which have both a structural and decorative function; Gaudí was in fact asked to come up with an original and inventive approach while being held to rigid cost limitations, something to which he was unaccustomed. The results were brilliant, precisely because of the enforced essentiality.

Solid yellow and red terracotta bricks were used for the window frames, the mitred arches, the cusps, the divisions between storeys and the framing for the bare ochre-coloured stone. There is a continuous blending of elements functional to the load-bearing structure and those of a decorative nature, which sometimes border on the over-elaborate. Very thin divisions between storeys at the front and back highlight the play of light and shade, and the precision of the proportions lends homogeneity to the whole building.

Pinnacles in terracotta rise from the building's four corners. Each one has a shelf supporting a spiral, skilfully laid brick column, at the centre of which is a ceramic shield bearing the symbols of the order: Mount Carmel surmounted by a cross, the heart of the Virgin with a crown of thorns and that of St Teresa pierced by arrows. The four high corner points are each topped with ceramic crosses, the arms of which are oriented towards the cardinal points. The initials of the religious order, S.H.S., in dark-red, glazed ceramic, recur throughout the string course of the four façades. The entrance portico is dominated by a triple, wrought-iron gate featuring geometric and botanical designs as well as Teresian symbols.

The masterly technical and compositional solutions on the outside are matched by a breathtakingly evocative inside, which is divided into three sections. The central one is primarily designed to confer ease of vertical and horizontal movement as well as to allow light and ventilation into the building. Gaudí always threw himself enthusiastically into resolving such technical challenges. Many scholars believe the building to be a metaphor for *Il castello interiore*, a mystical work by Teresa of Avila in which the saint compares the soul to a castle whose centre radiates the light of the divine presence.

Exterior of the college
Protruding from the front is the unit housing the entrance portico; in the centre of the outside wall is the crest with the symbols of the religious order of St Teresa.

Period photo of classroom

Gaudí made skilful use of building techniques to create two internal, well-lit open courtyards, the soul of this convent castle, flanked length-wise by corridors roofed by closely-placed catenary-section cross lancet arches, some of which rest on very slender pillars, often merely the thickness of a single brick. The light spreads over the white plaster surfaces of the arches, which contrast starkly with the dark terracotta pillars and flooring. From the ground floor to the roof (which can be accessed), the solid-brick, load-bearing structure was conceived as a dense and sturdy cross-weave frame to protect the central, vertical areas into which light pours from the side windows.

View of first-floor corridor with a sequence of tall catenary arches

1889 – 1893 · Palacio Episcopal
Astorga (León)

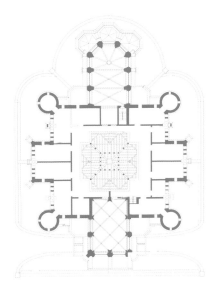

Plan of the main floor
The rooms are laid out around a large, central, full-elevation hall.

View of the side of the Palacio Episcopal, with the protruding apse of the chapel, in turn surrounded by three smaller apses

Facing page:
Dining room on the main floor

In 1886, Joan Baptista Grau i Vallespinós, a priest from Reus (where Gaudí was also born), was appointed to be the Bishop of Astorga in the province of León. Since the town did not have an appropriate building, he asked his fellow townsman, who by this time was well-known throughout Spain, to design a new bishop's palace.

Gaudí was fully occupied by his work on Palau Güell and the Sagrada Família – so he asked for photographs of the site that his friend, the bishop, had selected, only coming to Astorga when work was already underway.

The San Fernando Academy of Fine Arts, the body designated to supervise public buildings and in particular their artistic content, soon raised objections to many of Gaudí's neo-Gothic proposals, and when Grau died unexpectedly in 1893, Gaudí abandoned the project entirely.

The building is a vowedly neo-Gothic and was designed by Gaudí as a castle, constructed from substantial blocks of granite and surrounded by a moat. The central unit is square with four cylindrical towers at each corner, and smaller annexes protrude from each of its four sides. All the rooms develop round one large, double-storey room lit by skylights, and Mudéjar battlements are set into the strong, pyramid-shaped roof. The most complex of the rooms is the apse of the chapel, which is surmounted by three smaller apses, while the most evocative is the portico that features three high, pointed splayed arches with large keystones, and which are divided by leaning buttresses. On its external pinnacle, Gaudí planned to place a five-metre zinc angel. The inside rooms and décor originally inspired by Gaudí freely interpret Gothic stylistic themes and figures. The walls are plastered and graffito-decorated while motifs in dark-red glazed ceramic decorate the corners of the ceiling vaults. The capitals are unusually shaped, in some cases drawing inspiration from botanical themes, while others result from plays on volumes. There are also numerous, original stained-glass windows.

Designed as a residence with official apartments, it was never used as a bishop's palace and was soon turned into a museum. It was completed between 1907 and 1914 by the architect Ricardo García Garreta, who made a number of radical modifications, particularly in the upper parts, dividing the rooms and making additions to the building. Unfortunately, the homogeneity of the original design was lost as a consequence.

1891 – 1894 · Casa Fernández y Andrés

Plaza de San Marcelo, León

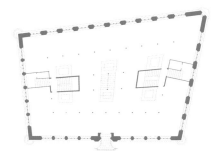

Ground-floor plan of the house

This building, designed for commercial use on the ground and lower-ground floors and for residential purposes on the upper three floors, occupies an entire trapezium-shaped city site near León Cathedral.

The owners, Mariano Andrés and Simón Fernández, friends of Eusebi Güell, were wholesale fabric dealers seeking a residence with high representational prestige. Gaudí designed a neo-Gothic building for them with rusticated granite façades. He embellished the four corners of the irregular rectangle with very prominent bow-window towers that had extremely steep tops, clad, like the pitched roof, in slate.

The compact volume is marked clearly by the projecting string course and the stone-framed attic windows giving on to the street. On the ground floor, the building is surrounded by a metal railing with breaks for two entrances on adjacent sides. This railing, made of a network of iron strips wrought in spiral form into rhombi, acts as protection for the basement while allowing an uninterrupted view of the building.

The static structure of the basement and ground floor is a frame of iron columns and beams, while the perimeter walls are in solid brick. This makes it possible for two floors to be completely free of load-bearing walls, because the slender iron columns provide sufficient support. These floors, designed for commercial use, have a separate entrance from the apartments, whose static structure, by contrast, consists entirely of load-bearing walls resting on the iron structure below.

In erecting this building, Gaudí availed himself of an expert team of Catalan masons led by Claudi Alsina, a master-builder he completely trusted and who had worked with him on Casa Vicens and was later to do so on the Sagrada Família.

The main entrance is dominated by a stone sculpture of St George slaying the dragon, executed by Gaudí's friend, Llorenç Matamala; he prepared the plaster model on the Sagrada Família site to the architect's instructions and under his watchful eye. When the statue was taken down for restoration in 1951, a lead tube was found behind it. Inside were the original designs for the whole complex, signed by Gaudí.

Facing page:
Central part of the front of the building, with the entrance portal overlooked by the large-scale sculpture of St George slaying he dragon

1898–1900 · Casa Calvet

Carrer Casp, 48, Barcelona

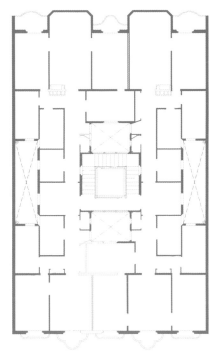

Plan of the second floor
The stairwell is wrapped around the lift shaft in the centre.

Facing page:
Lift, closed off by a wrought-iron gate and encircled by the stairs

This building marks the end of an exploratory compositional phase during which Gaudí interpreted, in a personal and "reasoned" fashion, as he himself put it, historical styles ranging from the romantic to Mudéjar, Gothic and baroque. It is unusually symmetrical and is the embodiment of a very reined-in neo-baroque tempered with a modernist sensibility, which may be seen in many ways.

Gaudí was commissioned by the children of Pere Màrtir Calvet, a textile industrialist, to construct a building with warehouse and shop premises in the basement and on the ground floor, a master apartment on the first floor and six apartments for renting on the upper three floors. The architect scrupulously followed the regulations on residential building laid down in the Eixample urban plan for the expansion of Barcelona, drawn up by Ildefons Cerdà in 1859. The plan stated that residential buildings had to be built on the outer edge of equal-sized blocks that were rectangular in shape with rounded corners. This would leave room for a garden in the middle. Generally speaking, the buildings had a rectangular plan and there were staircases inside. The day and night quarters had to be arranged along the two main sides, while the bathrooms, kitchens and store rooms could be placed in the centre of the building together with the ventilation shafts, or even adjacent to the stairs. The plan was also for the first floor to be completely occupied by the master apartment, while the higher floors could be divided into two apartments or more.

Gaudí's construction, along the main road in the heart of Eixample, has five floors above ground. The main façade of the ground floor has five large apertures, the central one of which is topped by a small but richly decorated tribune that stands out from the rusticated sandstone block facing, as do the five regular vertical rows of balconies. These are of two distinct shapes: some have a wide, single-stone, three-lobed base set atop a sculpted bracket, while others protrude very little. Both types of balcony are protected only by sturdy, wrought-iron bands worked into spirals and curled into scrolls. Below the tribune above the main entrance is carved the initial of the owner's surname, a cypress tree to symbolize hospitality and the crest of Catalonia. The tribune, by contrast, features carvings of various kinds of mushroom in the lower part, while the upper portion has symbols representing Amalthea's horn of plenty, overflowing with all kinds of fruit. Wrought-iron work, curled and folded into spirals, mesh with the stone sculptures.

The top of the façade is baroque with rounded cresting. The lower parts have busts of St Ginesio of Arles and Rome, and St Peter the Martyr, patron saint of the owner; the stone-carved heads have ray-shaped crowns in wrought iron. At the centre of the rounded masonry crest there are two minute balconies with hoists for raising the furniture from the street to the apartments, and at the very top there are stone supports to hold small, wrought-iron crucifixes.

The rear façade is also interesting, with its protruding verandas and balconies in stone; however, these are not in the neo-Gothic idiom but are modernist in style. The load-bearing structure of the building is of the traditional kind, comprising outer walls

Facing page:
Street façade
Perfectly aligned with the adjoining buildings,
it is topped by tall Baroque-style gables.

The tribune seen in profile
A drawing by Gaudí with a study for a coat of
arms to be inserted underneath the first floor.

**Ground-floor space, once a storeroom, now a
restaurant**
The wood walls, with shelves, crests and cornices,
are original and were designed by Gaudí.

in stone and interior ones in solid brick. The ceiling of the floors earmarked for the extensive warehouse space are slabs supported by long metal beams. Those of the residential floors, on the other hand, are small brick vaults supported on iron crossbeams and covered by wooden coffering.

Great care went into the design of the lift cabin in the entrance and its metal gate, flanked by small granite balusters and spiralled pillars. The stairwell, with its laminated iron banister, rises around the elevator shaft. The metalwork of the banister itself takes the form of a meshed network of concentric, intertwining circles. The bronze and iron doorframes are highly elaborate. Gaudí himself designed many of the furnishings and furniture in the master apartment and the proprietor's office; the chair, divan and oak desk have become famous for their functional simplicity, sturdiness and workmanship. The ground floor still has a number of the original dividing walls in wood and glass, which now enclose the elegant dining area of a restaurant.

In June 1900 the municipality of Barcelona awarded the building first prize for architecture, judging it to be the most attractive, original, functional and technologically up-to-date construction that year. For his part, Gaudí put a lot of energy into designing even the smallest details and thought carefully about what he wanted to achieve, not only with numerous drawings but also by using a plaster model, later subject to modifications, the last of which took place on site when construction work was already in progress.

1898–1915·Cripta de la Colònia Güell

Santa Coloma de Cervelló (Barcelona)

Ground plan of the columned hall in front of the entrance to the crypt, with sections of the roof construction and buttresses

Facing page:
Windows of the crypt, in multi-coloured lead glass
The windows open inwards in sections, like the petals of a flower or butterfly wings.

The crypt of the church of the Colònia Güell, in Santa Coloma de Cervelló near Barcelona, is rightly considered one of Gaudí's masterpieces. He started planning it in 1898 at the request of Count Güell, who had already had his architect friend Francesc Berenguer prepare an urbanization project for a workers' village linked to one of his textile factories. The church was sited on a hill on the edge of the village and set a little apart from the houses and factory buildings. Gaudí initially thought of doing a free interpretation of the Church of the Holy Sepulchre in Jerusalem, a concept dear to him, but which he was never able to bring to fruition in his life.

The method Gaudí developed to work on the design of this project, a wire model hung from his studio ceiling, is well known. Furthermore, in building the church – which remained incomplete –, he was also eager to test realization techniques and static-structural forms he had invented, with a view to applying them on a larger scale in the Sagrada Família.

Here he adopted a centralized plan in the shape of an irregular ovoid, closer to an ellipse than a circle. His plan was for a vertical development with strong, high towers of differing heights that would overlook a unitary, roughly cylindrical body. Using verification calculations, he pragmatically decided to develop a load-bearing structure that would not need buttresses or rampant arches, as Gothic architecture did, but was more similar to self-supporting shell forms found extensively in nature. In order to study this structure and its static capacity, he built a model comprising a web in hemp rope to which he attached lead-filled sacks, which he then hung from the ceiling of one of the huts on site. All that remains of this model, which has since been reconstructed by various European scholars, is a photograph in a 1929 book by the architect Josep Francesc Ràfols i Fontanals.

The ropes suspended from the ceiling enabled Gaudí to reproduce in 1:10 scale the combination of catenary curves to be used in defining the church's columns and arches. The walls and vaults were emulated by canvas sheets laid across the arches. The lead-filled sacks represented, in proportion, the weight and position of the loads exerted on the structure. If one imagines the model turned upside down, the result is an architectural skeleton of self-supporting elements that make up a system of continuous pillars and ribs. Gaudí photographed it and drew over the upside-down image. The photograph was decorated and embellished to give him an initial outline of his church.

A few studies of this kind, which show the outside and inside of the building, have come down to us, scant documentation for what was a prolonged period of study that lasted perhaps some ten years. Gaudí was assisted in this research by his architect friend Francesc Berenguer, the engineer Eduardo Goetz and another architect, Josep Canaleta.

The crypt of the church, the only part actually built, was to be the building's foundation. Constructed between 1908 and 1915, it looks organic on the outside and blends in with its surroundings, aided by the choice of stone similar in colour to the iridescent

Stereometric model for the church, retouched by Gaudí to indicate the complete plastic form of the building

shade of the bark of pine trees. The building is also partially below ground level in the sloping hilly terrain. The portico in front is entirely open and has various kinds of pillars, some manufactured from a single block of stone, others built using bricks. All of them, however, are variously inclined so as to lie along the profile of the catenary-curve arches. The portico roof has a ruled-surface geometric shape and is broken by connecting ribs departing from the pillars.

The light in the crypt is dim and highly evocative, and the whole area is mysterious and, at the same time, primordial. There is a large central room surrounded by an ambulatory and the space is delimited by outside walls in brickwork and the series of inclined pillars. The crypt's twenty-two windows, in leaded stained glass, open inwards in shapes reminiscent of flower petals or butterfly wings.

Each part is manufactured either from solid, roughly hewn stone blocks or from bricks, formed into pillars, walls, ribs, vaults and surfaces of overlapping bricks executed according to the traditional Catalan construction technique. Four inclining pillars were made from rough blocks of basalt, with individual pieces being used for the base, trunk and capital.

Facing the worshippers' area is the presbytery, which has not retained the exact form originally planned by Gaudí. Behind the presbytery there is a deep, dark ambulatory where, as in the temple in Jerusalem, the Holy Sepulchre was to have been placed on a level eighteen steps higher than the presbytery.

The harmony of shape (planned by Gaudí in minute detail down to the holy water font, the pews and the kneeling stools), the expressive richness of its structure, the evocative atmosphere of a primordial but nevertheless Christian religiousness, the variety of decoration, the polychromy, and the geometrical ideas used in its construction make this small building arguably the best paradigmatic example of Gaudí's building ability and poetics.

The crypt building site

Facing page:
Reversed wire and counterweight model to illustrate the interior spatial-static effect, realized by Salvator Tarragó

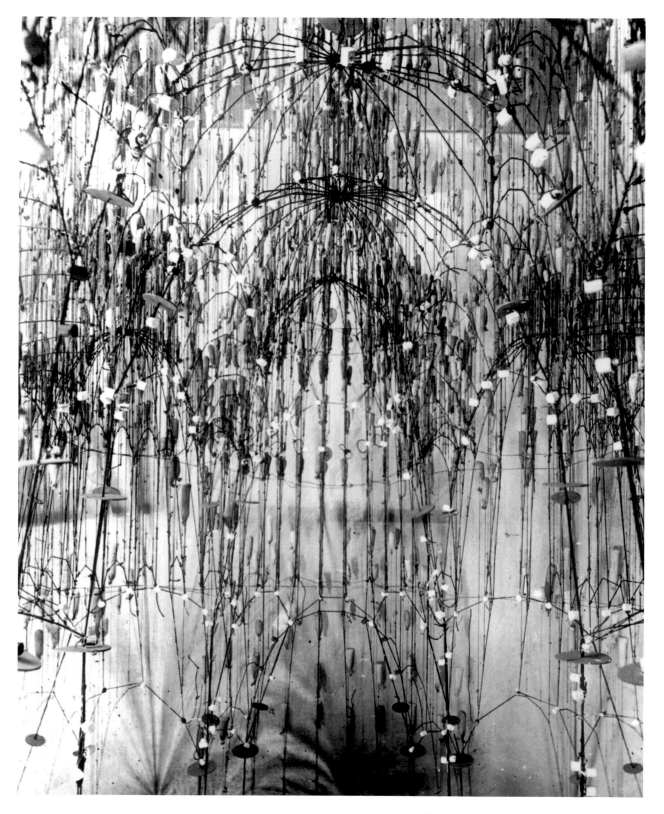

Interior of the crypt with a view of the presbytery and altar

In the foreground, an inclined column consisting of three blocks of rough-hewn stone. Above is the densely packed terracotta ribbing of the roof.

View of the portico in front of the crypt, showing the inclined pillars, ribbing and ruled-surface roof

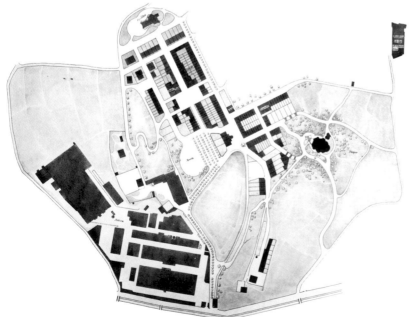

Exterior of the crypt
The portico in the foreground. In the background, sections of walling of an incomplete construction.

Plan of the Colònia Güell workers' quarter
The church is on a small hill separated from both the workers' houses and the factory units.

1900–1905 · Villa Bellesguard
Carrer Bellesguard, 16, Barcelona

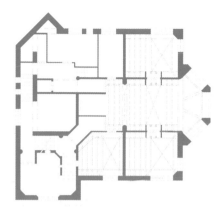

Ground-floor plan
The entrance hall, topped by the spire-viewing point, is on the sharp corner.

This building was a freely neo-Gothic Gaudí design incorporating the ruins of a medieval palace that had been the seat of the last monarch of the Catalan dynasty, Martín I el Humano, who died in 1410. The king's secretary, the poet Bernat Metge, gave it the name Bellesguard for the beautiful view it commanded. The king had personally had the garden planted with every type of flower and tree that grew in his kingdom. The land and ruins passed to the Bishop of Astorga and when he died in 1887 they were purchased by Maria Sagués, the widow of a food merchant, with the help of Gaudí, who signed the contract for her. She then gave Gaudí the job of building a house for her.

The memory of medieval Catalan glory and the legendary meekness of King Martín, as well as the beauty of the site, far from the city centre, spurred Gaudí to produce an original interpretation of Catalan civic Gothicism quite different from the sober austerity of the Col·legi de les Teresianes.

The villa is a compact cube rising vertically from a basement through the ground and main floors up to a very steep roof. On the west corner there rises a slim viewing spire topped by a cosmic crucifix with four equal arms decorated in coloured glass mosaic and oriented to the cardinal points. The sides of the building are faced with irregular pieces of slate of differing hues quarried from the site of the building itself.

The doors and windows are of different shapes, and are framed by prefabricated, moulded, geometric-shaped blocks of the same stone, or by reliefs made from pastes of local stone. These pastes were also used to decorate the twisting pillars of the upper gallery. Under the entrance spire there is a beautiful, wrought-iron gateway with the inscription "Ave Maria puríssima, sens pecat fou concebuda" (Hail Mary most Immaculate, conceived without sin).

For the general static construction Gaudí chose a load-bearing structure in solid brick, used also for the ceilings. Only some of the service rooms have a traditional beamed ceiling. The two floors with the living quarters have, by contrast, lowered vaults, those on the first floor being in the traditional Catalan, solid-brick tradition, layered like overlapping leaves.

The most surprising floor of the building is the *desván*, the first of two attic areas under the roof. All the load-bearing elements are in clearly visible brick; the structural layout is distinctly delineated and also has an effective decorative function. This square area has no internal dividing walls but is broken by eight central pillars which support a system of arches that underpin the under-roof ceiling as well as giving partial support to the roof load. Along the perimeter there are niches supporting the arches on which the very steep pitches of the roof rest. These niches provide the space for a perimeter walkway on the roof, which ends on the outside at the gallery above the façades, as well as allowing air and light into the room. Open, airy top-floor areas, possibly of rural origin, were still very common in Spain in Gaudí's time.

Gaudí stopped working on this building in 1903 and entrusted his architect friend Domènech Sugranyes with the task of finishing the decorative work. Sugranyes com-

View of the ceiling's ribbed structure

pleted the ceramic décor and bench feature surrounding the entrance portal as well as the lamp, railing and ceramic decoration on the stair. He also later added the covered portico and the custodian's house. On the other hand, Gaudí and another architect, Joan Rubió i Bellver, were responsible for rebuilding the ancient medieval walls and the small bridge in the garden.

Facing page:
Entrance hall, with the two short sets of stairs accompanied by vaguely neo-Gothic columns

1900 – 1914 · Park Güell

Carrer Olot, Barcelona

On returning from one of his frequent trips to England, where he had become familiar with the lively debate going on there at the time about garden-cities and the underlying principle of producing a blend of city and countryside, Eusebi Güell was fired with the idea of creating a prototype suitable for the Catalan bourgeoisie on land he owned on the outskirts of Barcelona. England had just started experimenting with worker garden-cities; the one at Letchworth set up by Ebenezer Howard was started in 1902.

Eusebi Güell did not, however, intend to build a worker garden-city immediately, a concept he implemented with the Colònia Güell. He was more interested in attracting the Barcelona bourgeoisie to this genre of urbanization, which was diametrically opposite to the compact city idea that had been launched by the Ensanche. He wanted his garden-city to be a luxurious private residential quarter enclosed by a substantial surrounding wall with just a few, carefully guarded entrances. He also wanted to set the houses in a sumptuous park of the kind created in 17th-century France, which he had seen in his youth.

In 1900, Güell asked Gaudí to draw up a general plan for a garden-city to be built on the 15-hectare area he owned on the side of the Muntanya Pelada, a bare, craggy hill whose name reflects its complete deforestation, which had deprived it of its Mediterranean vegetation. This rocky hill was part of the Serra de Collserola, exposed to the sun throughout the day. From the summit there is a view of the sea, the hinterland and the city.

Gaudí's idea was to subdivide the central part of the area into sixty, 1,100/1,200 m² lots; a third of each one could be built on. He drew up an exacting set of regulations regarding the construction of the residential buildings and the life of the park. Eusebi Güell immediately set the lots up for sale, but not before having organized both the structures for public use and the general utilities. This involved an electricity grid, nocturnal illumination of the park and the avenues through it, piping and telephone networks. Most of the area was set aside for a large park well equipped with public facilities – a market, a water tank, a church and a large open square for sports activities and open-air performances.

Gaudí and Güell's idea of a garden-city was not very popular with Barcelona's bourgeoisie. Just two lots were sold, one to the architect himself, who built a show house. It is likely that the failure of the project was due both to the overly restrictive building and management regulations and to the general lack of interest of the bourgeoisie, already busy building up the Eixample. The area did, however, attract groups and associations from Barcelona, who organized open-air performances and meetings. In 1906, before the hypostyle of the Greek temple was complete, the First Congress of the Catalan Language was held there; Gaudí was still highly active in various centres and, with Eusebi Güell, took an active part in movements favouring Catalan autonomy.

The only people who came to live in Park Güell were a lawyer named Trias and his descendants; Gaudí, his father and niece in 1906; and Count Güell, who lived from

Flights of stairs at the entrance to the park, providing direct access to the Doric temple or covered market
The multi-coloured iguana is probably an allusion to the python, in the central axis of the staircase, where flowers have been planted.

53

1906 to his death in 1922 in the pre-existing Larrand house which the architect had restructured for him. In 1923, Güell's son donated the park to the Barcelona municipal council, who turned it into a public park.

A number of Gaudí's architect friends assisted on work in the Park, including Jujol, Berenguer and possibly Rubió. The landscaping subsequently underwent numerous changes. In 1963 the Friends of Gaudí Association purchased the house he lived in and turned it into a museum. It was made a national monument in 1969 and in 1984 UNESCO declared it a World Heritage Site. In 1987, many areas of the Park were renovated by the architects Elies Torres i Tur and Josep Antoni Martínez i Lapeña.

The park shows Gaudí's flair for landscaping and was one of the ways in which he gave expression to his extensive knowledge of botany, which he had also pursued at university, attending optional courses in natural sciences and working extensively for the master-builder Josep Fontseré i Mestres, during the period when the latter was working on the Ciutadella, the first metropolitan public park. Fontseré had been commissioned to do the park after winning a competition in 1872, and the young Gaudí probably worked on the architectural structure of a receptacle below a waterfall. Fontseré interpreted the design of the park as a continuation of the idea of romanticism, exemplified by Barcelona's Laberint d'Horta garden from the late 18th century.

Gaudí wished to keep faith with this idea of romanticism though he added a strong Mediterranean naturalism of his own invention. He was very familiar with typical Mediterranean vegetation, its subtropical species and how the landscape looked when used for agriculture. He also had a strong drive to blend architecture and nature in various ways; the park is just one example of this, and can be seen in Park Güell and in the Jardins Artigas at La Pobla de Lillet, a project only recently attributed to him. The design of residential gardens, isolated or in urban settings, was a second, while a third was the ingenious attempt to transpose elements he had discovered in the natural world into stone. One example is the use of ruled surfaces, the catenary, which he found on the surfaces of leaves or tree-trunks. Another is the way his buildings blend into the surrounding landscape, of which the Colònia Güell crypt is a well-known example. And yet another is what may be called gardens in stone, as can be seen on the façade of the Nativity of the Sagrada Família, with its Catalan flowers and vegetation.

In the Park Güell project, Gaudí's landscaping ability is exemplary in many ways, first and foremost in the complexity of the layout of the internal pedestrian and vehicular thoroughfares, which he kept separate. These routes had to be designed with sinuous curves following the contours of the often steep, almost bare and rocky terrain, so as to avoid altering the shape with excavations. When the roadway was left hanging, he came up with terracing and viaducts. Strict observance of the need to preserve the features of the terrain stimulated him to invent grottoes similar to those found in nature and to place routes hard against earthwork, like the porticoes underpinned by inclined columns with their spiral or anthropomorphic trunks. In the open areas, he added to the scanty vegetation by introducing pines, carobs, oaks and palms, and allowed broom, rosemary and thyme to grow freely together with climbing plants like jasmine and wisteria.

The pathways in the park are organized around two main avenues that begin at the entrance. The main pedestrian walkway leads straight to the covered market square of the Doric temple by way of a broad double staircase. From there, it continues to the

View of the Park from above

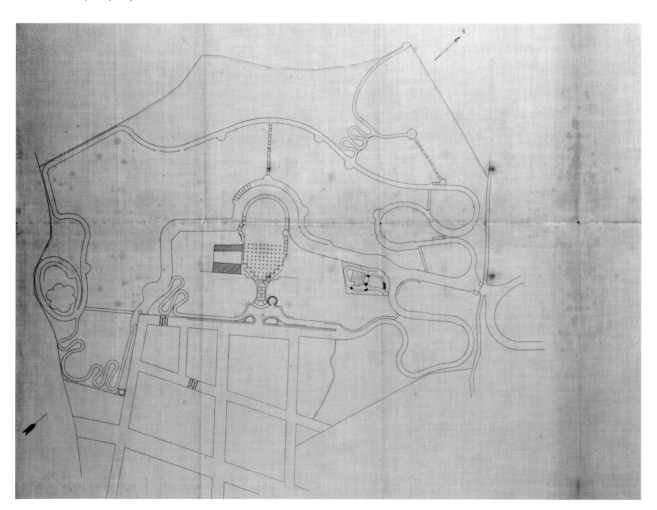

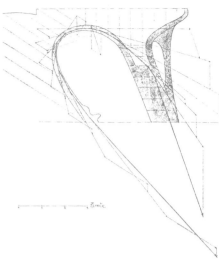

People in one of the colonnaded walkways, in 1904

Above right:
Graphic analysis of the statics of a portico beneath one of the viaducts in the park
The drawing may have been prepared in Gaudí's studio for the Paris Exposition in 1910, cat. no. 38.5.

large, upper square with its Greek theatre. This involves a sudden rise of 17 metres. Two other paths circle the park in opposite directions, joining together in the Park's upper reaches. From here, a series of long straight, steep stairways lead back down to the square of the Greek theatre. One of the two paths runs around the Calvario, the Park's highest point and the summit of an isolated promontory; there had been a plan to build a church but in the end three crosses were erected there. There are some 30 kilometres of paths in the Park. Three bridges are positioned at regular intervals along the viaduct sections, which provide protection for pedestrian pathways underneath.

In 1903, construction work began on the two buildings beside the entrance, the stairway protecting a large garage, the Doric temple (with a water-tank underneath) and the main square or Greek temple over it. The Greek temple was completed in 1906, the curved seating for the Greek theatre in 1914.

The gateway to the park was a simple wooden gate until 1965, when it was replaced by a wrought-iron gate with palm-tree designs that came from Casa Vicens. The Park's perimeter wall, 3.8 metres high, was built to prevent any intrusion. Constructed in masonry faced with irregular stones, it is slightly concave towards the base. The middle section, in uncut stone, was pointed and had a covering like an upended ship's hull a metre high and it was inset with ceramic fragments on top. At periodic intervals along this smooth and slippery upper part are large medallions in fragmented ceramic with the alternating inscription "Park" and "Güell". There is an opening in the wall for a vehicle access gate and a secondary entrance higher up in the park, at the top of a stairway.

The two buildings alongside the main entrance (the warden's house and park management premises) were clad with the same, deep ochre, rustic stone finishing as

Facing page:
Two levels of paths in the park
Delineated by roughly hewn stone, their forms blend with the surrounding Mediterranean vegetation.

Mosaic of ceramics and coloured crystal on a green background set into the white ceiling of the Doric temple

Detail of the columned hall

the surrounding wall. These buildings may have been inspired by Engelbert Humperdinck's opera *Hansel and Gretel*, which was playing at Barcelona's Liceu theatre at the time.

Just inside the entrance to the Park there is an iridescent, ceramic-clad staircase comprising two symmetrical stairways, each divided into three sections. Gaudí left a space between the two stairways, occupied by a rest area and a series of figures, which hide the water flowing downhill until it gushes from the fountains. The lowest basin has a Japanese garden in miniature, while at the mid-level the basin is surmounted by the heraldic shield of Catalonia, inlaid in a medal from which a mysterious serpent rises. The third fountain is dominated by an iguana reminiscent of Python, the mythical guardian of underground waters, from whose open mouth the water gushes. The water comes directly from a large 1,200-cubic-metre subterranean receptacle with mighty columns and arches.

The market, or Doric temple area is an evocative space with eighty-six sturdy Doric columns that underpin a roof of domes supported on slightly curved beams. Everything is lined with white ceramic reminiscent of the wave motion of the sea, thanks to a reverberation effect of the light, an effect heightened by the slight inclination of some of the columns. The ceramic lining features polychromatic circles in ceramic and crystal, with intertwined serpents. The temple roof was built by Gaudí using prefabricated terracotta components hidden behind a packed earth cladding. Alongside the temple there is a source of mineral water, which Eusebi Güell sold under his own name.

The square of the Greek theatre in packed earth is delimited by a long, continuous serpentine bench-balustrade. This bench structure is decorated in trencadís ceramic,

Serpentine seat enclosing the piazza, also known as the Greek theatre, which rests above the Doric temple
The long seat is covered by fragments of coloured ceramic. Gaudí's assistants included the architect Josep Maria Jujol.

and its sinuous shape has loops that can accommodate small groups of people. The side facing outwards joins the frieze of the Doric temple below, of which the upper part is decorated with gargoyles in the shapes of lions' heads. The decoration of the sinuous seat is celebrated because it is a forerunner of expressive means later used by artists like Miró, Picasso and Braque. In the band along the edge of the backrest, Gaudí inserted religious and pro-Catalan inscriptions and symbols, some of which were lost in the 1989 renovation.

Above left:
Gaudí's own house in the park

Above right:
The office building at the entrance to the park
The high tower crowned by a cross is the main landmark reference for the whole park.

Facing page:
Detail of the roof of the warden's building at the park entrance

1903–1914 · Catedral de Mallorca
Palma de Majorca, Majorca

Towards the end of the 19th century, the Bishop of Majorca, Pere Campins i Barceló, gave a lot of attention to the emergence in Roman Catholicism, and especially in the monastic context, of a movement calling for liturgical reform. What especially concerned him was the fact that a large stone choir for the canons of the Cathedral Chapter blocked the view to the altar and the presbytery from the longitudinal area where worshippers would gather.

Gaudí suggested eliminating the canons' choir in the main nave and using its parts to decorate the apse walls. He removed the two large decorative elements above the altar, called retabli, one Gothic and the other baroque. He also opened large windows in the royal chapel. He suggested installing a new high altar; moved the choir stalls and the choir to the back of the presbytery and transferred the two royal tombs of Jaime II and Jaime III of Majorca into the chapel of the Trinity. Highly ambitious and complex, the project also envisaged new stained glass windows and the installation of religious artefacts throughout the church.

It was not, however, fully completed; work moved forward slowly due to disagreements and difficulties until 1914. However, Gaudí had already withdrawn from the project some years previously, to dedicate his efforts to the Sagrada Família project.

With the help of local craftsmen and his faithful assistants, in particular Jujol, Gaudí dismantled the choir and other parts, which he then reassembled in a free style in the presbytery around a new altar he had designed. The two most important new works he produced are the sumptuous multi-level lamp-holder cum canopy at the centre of the presbytery, richly decorated in symbolic figures, and the windows of the royal chapel invoking the Virgin of Loreto. In these, he succeeded in creating a particularly contemporary effect by using superimposed stained glass with abstract figures and designs.

Below left:
Wood and wrought-iron predella, designed by Gaudí

Below right:
Crown of wrought-iron chandeliers around a polygonal pillar in the cathedral, designed by Gaudí

Facing page:
View of the presbytery inside the cathedral
In the foreground, the main altar, a simple surface with a baldacchino-lamp above, both designed by Gaudí.

1904–1906 · Casa Batlló
Passeig de Gràcia, 43, Barcelona

Plan of the main floor
This shows the central patio with the stairs and lifts. The building occupies a long, narrow plot further narrowed by two other residential buildings.

Facing page:
View of the main façade from the street

In 1904, Gaudí and his friend and entrepreneur Josep Bayó i Font, a successful building contractor who later also built the Casa Milà, were commissioned to renovate a small building on a rectangular plot of land along the Passeig de Gràcia, which at that time was the city's main road artery. Most of the buildings by leading modernist Catalan architects were also constructed in this period. Next door stood the interesting Casa Amatller, with its stepped top, designed by Josep Puig i Cadafalch, a famous architect also internationally known as a historian of architecture.

Gaudí enlarged the basement, added a fifth floor for the servants' quarters and completely renovated the main floor where the Batlló family lived. He enlarged and renovated the patio or central covered courtyard in order to admit more light, renewed the external façades and built a new roof covering. The plan of the remaining floors was left untouched.

The façade facing the street – the one most admired – is in grey sandstone carved with botanical motifs at ground- and first-floor levels. These form a sturdy, protruding base rising into a generous tribune at main floor level. This base also wraps around the load-bearing structure for the whole façade, six stone pillars connected by five arches. The concave and convex volumetric movement is reminiscent of boned structures and emphasizes the sense of solidity and sturdiness. Above the first two floors there is an iridescent polychromatic façade which has a slightly undulating effect due to the use of glazed ceramic. The mosaic was personally supervised by Gaudí, and involved the use of some two hundred ceramic discs in three different sizes and thicknesses placed into a base of ceramic fragments with colours matching those of the discs. The predominant colour is a shiny blue-green, the hue of which changes throughout the day. Its lightness and irregularity is in pleasant contrast to the regular spacing of the windows and the severe cast-iron parapets of the balconies, which are shaped into small masks.

The undulation is accentuated near the corners adjacent to the Casa Amatller, helping the turret that protects the spiral staircase giving on to the roof to emerge more fully; this turret is also covered with discs and fragmented ceramic. Gaudí initially wanted to set the turret at the centre of the high part of the façade, now occupied by a small, attractive balcony in wrought iron that has a winch for raising furniture to the floors. By moving the turret to the side, he managed to achieve a clever and harmonious relationship, by adding a small terrace, with the façade designed by Puig i Cadafalch. Standing out from its cylindrical volume are the acronyms in enamelled ceramic of Jesus, Joseph and Mary, a devotional tribute to the Holy Family. The facing ends at the mansard roof with its double under-roof, a habit of Gaudí's, which afforded good protection against temperature swings as well as providing excellent ventilation. The asymmetrical animal-form crest on the roof, with its marked upward sweep, is reminiscent of a dragon's back. This is clad in scale-tiling made of glazed ceramic in colours ranging from yellow to green and light blue.

Scholars of Gaudí's work are unanimous in acknowledging this façade as one of Gaudí's greatest compositional triumphs. Here he achieved a clever balance between

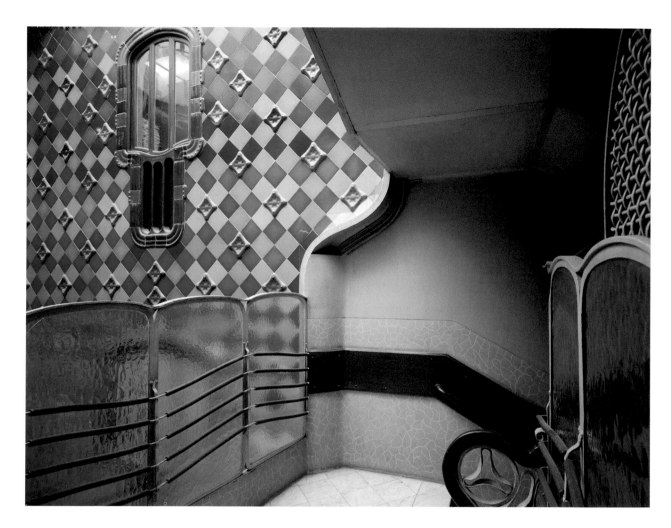

different and independent elements – the materials used, the relationship between interior and exterior, the irregular modular components and the constant play of asymmetric forms. The overall effect of unity is also stunning, a single, vibrating entity that changes constantly in the light.

Today's façade is the last version of Gaudí's plan, only completed when work was already in progress on site. Scholars recall that Gaudí spent a long time working on a plaster model of the whole building, and the surface undulation of the façade only appeared towards the end after a lot of trial, error and correction. The mask-like, cast-iron parapets of the balconies were also developed by using a 1:1 scale plaster model.

The entrance to the building is on the far left of the façade as one looks at it. Once inside, there are two possible routes. The first leads straight to the stairs that give access to the main floor where the master apartment is located, while the second crosses the patio and leads up two flights of stairs winding round the open lift shaft to the rented apartments and the servants' quarters. The lift shaft is at the centre of the patio illuminated by light coming in from the double-pitched roof through a skylight set in a parabola-shaped iron support. Alongside this are a number of fixed apertures provid-

View of the central patio well on the top floor, with stairs and lifts
To soften the light streaming in from the skylight, Gaudí faced the walls with deep blue ceramic tiles.

Detail of the banisters

ing natural ventilation; the air is forced to rise in much the same way as happens with a normal fireplace chimney.

The patio walls, into which the windows of the apartments on the various floors are set, are lined with white and light blue ceramic tiles arranged in a diagonal pattern to create a sense of spaciousness. The tiles are a deep shade of light-absorbing blue at the top, becoming progressively lighter as they descend until they are white at the bottom. The windows are surrounded by unusually shaped bi-chromatic ceramic frames.

The Batlló family apartment on the main floor is reached by a vestibule on the ground floor that has a wooden staircase, the edging of which is carved into a sinuous, hugging spinal form. The walls, too, have a wavy surface up to a second vestibule by the entrance, lit by two windows let into the ceiling. The Batlló apartment is laid out with a number of various-sized rooms with undulating walls and ceilings, thereby conveying the idea of a fluid continuum of space.

A waiting room in the entrance hall with a dark ceramic fireplace set into the wall gives on to a large living room in which an undulating wooden screen conceals an altar. A big wooden partition decorated with coloured glass can open like a concertina to link

67

Detail of the front of the building

the lounge with the room behind it. The dining room, by contrast, looks out of the sunny, rear part of the building onto a wide terrace-garden livened by ceramic decorations.

The rear of the building is protected and decorated on all the floors by strongly undulating iron-work parapets, the edges and top of which are decorated by slivers of coloured ceramic.

From 1936–1939, the building was used as a refugee centre during the Civil War. It was sold to an insurance company in 1940, which carried out a first restoration. It later passed into private ownership.

Vertical section of the building along the longitudinal axis
The patio is in the centre. To the rear, the terrace of the main floor.

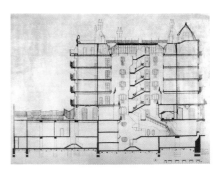

1906–1910 · Casa Milà

Passeig de Gràcia, 92, Barcelona

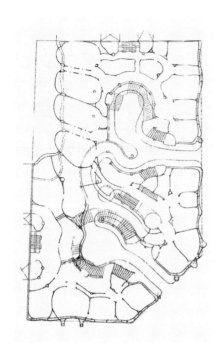

Plan of the ground floor with the two inner courtyards
Around them are grouped the irregularly shaped rooms of the four apartments.

Facing page:
View of the main façade of the corner house
Up above, the double wave profile with protruding chimneys and the bell-shaped staircase-exits on the roof terrace.

Visiting the interior of Casa Milà, and the nearby Casa Batlló, walking up and down the stairs and round the apartments, one's gaze falls onto walls stirred by waves and gorges, on doors and windows in curved wood and coloured glass, on brass handles that seem to have been made from hand-clenched wax casts, on ceilings in shaped plaster, on the numerous hand-crafted and surprisingly valuable furnishings and fixtures. The sensation is one of being pleasantly immersed in the fluid cavity of a gigantic body, rendered warm and hospitable by continuous contrasts of light and colour obtained through the use of a wide range of building materials. In the interior decoration of Casa Milà there is a prevalence of ornamental marine themes, which accentuate this sense of fluid continuity. The ceilings, in particular, are finished with broad waves of moulded plaster that simulate the movement of water, sometimes ruffled by the wind, sometimes wrapped into spirals which recall the eddies and curls of foam on the sea shore. There are etched polyp and marine flora patterns here and there, together with sea snails in relief.

Casa Milà was commissioned by Pere Milà i Camps and Roser Segimon i Artells. Located on the corner between Passeig de Gràcia and Carrer Provença, the site had previously been occupied by a small chalet and was on the edge of the municipalities of Barcelona and Gràcia, which fused in 1897.

Six stories high, with eight apartments on each floor grouped around two internal courtyards, one circular and the other oval, it was a costly and complex construction in keeping with the owner's ambitions. The building immediately aroused fierce criticism and ironic comment, widely reported in the papers. Humorous magazines compared it to a large futurist garage for airships.

It has a large rectangular plan pierced in the centre by two big courtyards; the polygonal outer walls are moulded with light plastic reliefs and are completely frescoed with abstract or vegetable and floral motifs on a mottled background where the blotches, mainly red, blue and yellow, blend into each other. The static structure consists of solid bricks and stone pillars. The dividing walls are not load-bearing, so the size of the apartments varies constantly from floor to floor. In the basement is a large iron pillar, radiating out from which are iron beams that support the circular courtyard above, around which Gaudí wanted to site a garage.

Gaudí devoted a great deal of energy to planning the façade and moulding it in stone, as his drawings demonstrate. Initially he thought in terms of elevations similar to those of Casa Batlló, with a traditional and regular pattern of balconies and galleries. In a plaster model presented at the Paris Exposition in 1910, the façade with two adjoining fronts had already taken on plastic, heaving forms. Gaudí managed to invent a load-bearing structure whose functions were to support only itself and to close the space, to be, therefore, no longer a load-bearing wall but a curtain wall. The gently undulating line of the upper profile of the façade is broken at a number of points by minute sculptures in rose-bud forms next to Latin texts in relief, which are easily legible in some points from the road.

View into the inner courtyard

The large architectural volume of the façade, which slopes inwards towards the crown of the building, has the appearance of a single mass, thanks to the powerful undulating relief of the surface across which daylight plays freely. The surface is made from blocks of stone anchored by iron clamps to a normal internal brick wall. The positioning of these blocks was carefully supervised by Gaudí so that the undulations fit visually into surface units. These blocks, which came from the mountains of El Garraf and Vilafranca del Penedès, gave rise to the Casa Milà's nickname of 'La Pedrera', meaning 'quarry'.

The wrought iron on the balconies is shaped into abstract and botanical motifs characterized by undulating, sinuous leaves. The iron work forms a kind of sculptural collage that was realized in the Barcelona workshop of the Badia brothers under the direct supervision of Gaudí. There is a spectacular main entrance gate, a curvilinear weft of iron leaving space for pieces of glass that are smaller at the bottom and larger at the top. For the pavement on the road below and for some interior spaces, Gaudí designed a floor of hexagonal ceramic tiles with polyp, star and snail motifs in slight relief, realized by a company called Escofet. Gaudí concerned himself with every minor detail, including the bronze door handles, which correspond perfectly to the movements of the hand and are excellent to handle. The wood fixtures in the lifts and on the doors also have a plastic sculptural relief.

Cartoon from a daily paper, deriding Casa Milà, which is compared to an aircraft and airship hanger
In *L'Esquella de la Torratxa*, Barcelona, 1912.

Above right and below:
Wrought-iron work on the balconies protruding from the main elevations
For this, sheets of iron were used that were bent, entwined, pierced and overlain into mainly abstract forms, though there are sometimes allusions to human, botanical and animal forms.

There is an atmospheric, practicable roof with horizontal undulations. This roof is dotted with stair exits covered by white trencadís ceramics; spiral-shaped ventilation towers, decorated at the top with fragments of dark-green bottle glass; as well as chimneys, on their own or in groups of three or four, each topped by a small dome structure. The stair units are surmounted by crosses with four equal arms; those of the chimneys by small domes similar to warriors' helmets. It is known that the whole set of features was prepared by Gaudí in a plaster model, with the assistance of the sculptor Bertran, on a scale of 1:10. Additional chimneys were subsequently removed during restoration in 1995. The practicable roof of Casa Milà carries a powerful emotive charge, and visitors feel they have been plunged into a mysterious dialogue between masked characters in a fluid space that has all the characteristics of a dream but is actually material reality.

When Gaudí, by then a mature, established architect, received the commission to design this vast, upper-middle class residential complex, he imbued it with religious symbolic meanings, initially accepted by the client but later rejected out of fear of heated reaction from anarchic and anticlerical movements in Barcelona.

In particular, Gaudí wanted the building to become the gigantic base for a monumental sculptural group in stone, gilded metal and crystal, consisting of two large angels and a 25-metre-high statue of the Virgin of the Rosary, to be positioned on the

Interior of a room in the owner's apartment on
the main floor, with the original furnishings,
now lost

**Solid, ergonomic and modernist bench from
the owner's apartment**
Designed by Gaudí between 1906 and 1910.

Chimney and stair unit on a roof terrace

roof of the house. The three figures would have dominated the city, emerging from the undulating profile of the long façade (inscribed with words from the Hail Mary) to occupy a position between the chimneys and the solid stair units. As we see it today, the façade is unfinished. In fact, Gaudí did not complete the construction of the building due to strong disagreements that arose around 1910 with Pere Milà's wife.

In the following years, the building underwent numerous modifications; in 1946 it was sold to the estate agency Provença, who in 1954–55 commissioned the architect Barba Corsini to create thirteen apartments in the attic area. In 1966, the architect Gil Nebot transformed the main floor into offices for a foreign company. The first restoration work, much of it questionable, was carried out between 1971 and 1975 under the supervision of the architect Josep Antoni Comas. In 1986 the Caixa de Catalunya purchased the building in order to refurbish it and use it as a cultural centre open to the public. The Casa was restored again between 1987 and 1996; the work was rounded off by restoration of the walled attic, consisting of sequences of hyperbolic paraboloid arches which develop in serpentine patterns around the cylindrical volumes of the stairs. Built using the Catalan technique, these arches are in rows of just one brick and are joined together by ribs, also of just one brick, supporting the undulating roof.

Known throughout the world, Casa Milà was officially listed as part of the artistic heritage of Barcelona in 1962, and has been a UNESCO World Heritage Site since 1984.

Facing page:
Aerial view of the atmospheric roof terrace
It is laid out around the circular and ovoidal
courtyards. The stair units, air ducts and
chimneys (on their own or in groups) are all
clearly visible.

**Attic with catenary arches in one of the
apartments set up here in the 1960s**
This was returned to its original state during
restoration work carried out between 1987 and
1996.

1909 · Classrooms of the Sagrada Família
Carrer Sardenya and Carrer Mallorca, Barcelona

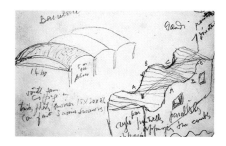

Undulating roof of the school or perhaps of Gaudí's workshop (no longer extant), drawn by Le Corbusier in a page of his notebook, probably during a visit to Barcelona towards the end of the 1930s
There is also a note on the Catalan vault, subsequently drawn upon in a number of signficant projects from the 1950s onwards.

This small building, regarded by Gaudí as provisional, was commissioned in 1909 by the Associació Espiritual de Devots de Sant Josep, which promoted the construction of the Sagrada Família. It was sited on free land destined, however, to be occupied by the façade of the Gloria of the large church, which is only now, in 2002, beginning to be erected. The small brick construction has recently been moved further out, though it is still on the corner between Carrer Sardenya and Carrer Mallorca. In a poor condition due to damage caused during the Civil War of 1936–1939, it was recently dismantled in blocks, carefully rebuilt and restored. Domènech Sugranyes i Gras had already rebuilt it in the 1940s, with the limited funds available, restoring the roof in particular. Due to subsequent collapses, the architect Francesc Quintana also carried out another reconstruction in 1943, altering the original project to some extent, replacing the original wooden bars with steel ones, strengthening the interior with double walls and dividing the space into smaller rooms than the ones envisaged by Gaudí.

The Escoles are built entirely from full bricks laid in three layers that overlap like leaves, in the Catalan fashion. Both the walls and the roof have ruled spatial surfaces and are light, stable and resistant. In the design of this temporary structure, he came up with a coherent static structure defined by specialists as resistant, thanks to the form of the cladding itself. This is an extremely compact, self-supporting shell, a rigid skin deriving from its undulating shape; although very thin it is very resistant.

Gaudí was fifty-seven in 1909, and was working on Casa Milà and Park Güell; he was also in the process of studying his stereostatic models, which used wires and counterweights, for the church of Santa Coloma de Cervelló. He was at the peak of his professional maturity, intensely engaged in the invention of new building solutions.

The only decorative features are above the window openings: triangular-shaped relief motifs in terracotta that also offer protection from the rain. He divided the space outside into three areas – which are still visible and once acted as open-air classrooms –, using iron pergolas covered with straw matting. The small building is a 10- by 20-metre rectangle, originally divided into three separate classrooms running diagonally. There was also an entrance hall and a chapel. The bathrooms were in a protruding structure.

The constructive simplicity and originality of the building attracted the attention of many contemporary architects, who were amazed by its geometric purity and rigorous functionality. The influence of the successful, plastically modelled roof can be traced in the works of Le Corbusier, Eduardo Torroja, Pier Luigi Nervi, Félix Candela and Santiago Calatrava. Le Corbusier produced a signed sketch during a visit to Barcelona at the end of the 1930s, probably of the roof covering Gaudí's studio workshop, no longer in existence but which at the time was also on the corner between Carrer Sardenya and Carrer Provença.

This second, ruled-surface building, constructed like the Escoles in the Catalan manner, was begun in 1887 and completed, following a number of enlargements, in 1906. This was Gaudí's base for his work as Director of Works of the Sagrada Família site. This is where he designed many of his masterpieces from 1887 onwards and where

Facing page:
View from above of part of the small school

Classroom, 1913

he collected all his designs and plaster models. Unfortunately the building was completely destroyed by a fire in 1936 during the Civil War. The whole collection of documents was completely burnt, and many of the plaster models seriously damaged. What survived the devastation has been painstakingly restored. The last remnants of the building, on other hand, were completely dismantled recently.

Despite its extremely modest size, the Escoles are now considered worthy of the fullest possible restoration to conserve it, because it is an exemplary example of Gaudí's masterly genius in the use of traditional building techniques combined with highly plastic geometric-structural solutions. The possibility of inventing new spaces – organic and essential at the same time – offered by the use of ruled surfaces is in fact clearly evident in this building.

The effective blending of tradition and innovation is a typical expression of Gaudí's overall work and can be found in many highly complex forms in the crypt of the church of Colònia Güell and in the Sagrada Família design. However, it is easier to grasp here than elsewhere, and the Escoles can therefore rightly be viewed both as a building manifesto of Gaudí's inventiveness and an unmatched prototype of organic spatiality and curvilinear modulation.

The newly-built school in the foreground; in the background, the spires of the apse of the Sagrada Família

Elevation of the school

1883–1926 · Sagrada Família
Plaça de la Sagrada Família, Barcelona

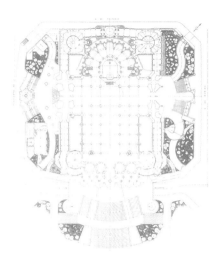

Plan of the church according to the definitive scheme drawn up by Gaudí and published in 1929
The Latin cross is surrounded on three sides by a portico. Gaudí proposed three large entrance portals, like in the Gothic cathedral of Chartres.

The votive temple of the Sagrada Família takes its name from the fact that it is dedicated to Jesus Christ and his earthly parents, Joseph and Mary, who together comprise the ideal model of the Christian family. Gaudí became chief architect and Director of Works in 1883. Only gradually and prudently, especially at first, did he reinterpret and rework the design of his predecessor, Francesc de Paula Villar i Lozano. He was regretful that he had to take account of the pre-established orientation of the structure, which could not be modified because construction of the crypt was already at an advanced stage. The orientation was along an axis that was diagonal in relation to the right-angled, square-grid pattern established in the Eixample plan. On the other hand, he was satisfied by its position in the centre of the new urban expansion on the plain of Barcelona, equidistant from the nearby rivers, the sea and the mountains inland.

Gaudí regarded churches as being the most representative buildings of a people, and so he decided to produce a spatial and figurative synthesis of its symbolic imagination. For this reason he filled the architectural forms with emblems, with figures of patron saints and of men of his age in the guise of biblical characters, and with Catalan features of flora and fauna. He also selected biblical episodes and religious texts, which formed key elements of an explanatory sculptural narration.

Although he kept in general to the design of his predecessor, Gaudí strongly accentuated the verticality of the construction with high towers. He also gave the wide Latin-cross plan – with a nave and four side aisles in the longitudinal section and three in the transept – three façades. Over each of these there rise four imposing bell-towers, with spiral staircases inside. The wing to the east of the transept is completed by the façade of the Birth, the one to the west by the façade of the Passion, while the main entrance, to the south, is part of the façade of the Glory. The sculptural symbolism of the three façades provides some very explicit religious instruction on the foundations of the Christian faith.

On the east one, the sculptures and stained glass celebrate the joy of the created world at the birth of Jesus; there are scenes from his childhood and adolescence. On the west one, the sculptures offer a dramatic illustration of the events of the Passion and the death of Christ, finishing with the inspiration of the Resurrection. On the side facing the sea is the main façade, still not complete today, which illustrates how humans can participate in Divine Glory and enjoy the fruits of the Redemption brought by Jesus Christ.

The space where the longitudinal nave meets the transept is covered by a large vault, above which there is an imposing tower or cimborio, topped by a tall tower-beacon with four equal cross arms 170 metres above the ground. Around this are four smaller towers symbolizing the four Evangelists; from their top, they too radiate light over the city. The bell tower above the apse is dedicated to the Mother of Christ and decorated with a crown of twelve stars. Eighteen towers are envisaged in all, eight of which have been built to date.

Facing page:
Cathedral with the façade of the Birth in the foreground

Wooden confessional

The bell towers of Gaudí's three façades are crowned by the representation of the attributes of the bishops, who succeeded the apostles – the cross staff, the mitre, the ring and the cross. A series of words on the cylindrical body of the towers – "Sanctus, Sanctus, Sanctus; Hosanna, Excelsis" – involves those reading them in the celebration of the glory of God. Overall, the building is representative of the Universal Church, heavenly and earthly. Gaudí's plan envisages that it must be entirely enclosed by a rectangular cloister that can be walked around. He has designed small buildings for sacristies and administrative offices at the corners of the cloister.

There are two fundamental principles to the construction logic and statics of the building. One is the parabolic curve of the vertical sections, which makes possible the upward rake of the interior spaces. The other is the shape of the pillar, inclined because it lies along the parabolic curve, and which is broken up into a number of branches, namely other, shorter-section inclined pillars, which support the vaults of the church, with large oculi at the top so the sky can be seen. These two principles, simultaneously static and formal, are the result of studies conducted by Gaudí on his stereostatic model, with its wires and counterweights, constructed for the church of Santa Coloma de Cervelló. In the construction system of the Sagrada Família, however, there is a new element, an inventive step forward on the static conception he developed for the church of Santa Coloma. This is the relation between the tree-like branching structure of the pillars and the ruled-surface geometry of the vaults. The delicate outcome of this can be seen in work carried out on the site during the final decades of the 20th century. Due to its complexity, Gaudí produced many models, to different scales, of various parts of the building, in order to achieve a "definitive transfiguration of the Gothic", concluding and moving beyond the architectural exploration of the great European medieval builders.

It is currently thought that Gaudí anticipated a number of his inventions and key images – fully expressed in the Sagrada Família – in an earlier project for Güell's brother-in-law, the Marqués de Comillas. The Marqués wanted to give the Franciscans a major centre for their missionary work, so he asked Gaudí to draw up a grandiose project for Tangiers in Africa. In his first sketches, in 1892–93, which remained on paper, he designed a multitude of bell towers similar to the ones found in the Sagrada Família. Gaudí constantly drew on a rich, carefully thought-out symbolism anchored to the medieval Catholic tradition, which was often allegorical because it was deliberately didactic.

Gaudí must have had a vivid memory of the imposing Gothic cathedrals of Tarragona, Barcelona, Palma de Mallorca, and all the cathedrals of the Iberian peninsula, which gave to European Gothic architecture an exuberant grandeur of dimensions and forms.

He was also well versed in the rites and symbols of Catholic liturgy. He studied the two-volume *L'Année liturgique* by the Benedictine monk Dom Guéranger on an almost daily basis. This gave him an insight into the meanings of liturgical furnishings, the symbolic value of colours used in decorations in various periods of the year and ways of celebrating the sacraments and Mass. Besides the religious connotations of his work, which he cultivated over the years with his own personal credo, nature always remained his major source of inspiration.

A project the size of the Sagrada Família takes a long time to complete, and in order to leave his successors a clear idea of his intentions, he decided, in the final years of

Full view of the cathedral based on a drawing
by Joan Rubió i Bellver published in 1906

his busy life, not to continue building the church in horizontal sections but to complete the vertical development of the Birth façade. This enabled him to see the first completed bell tower free from scaffolding in the final months of his life.

Moreover, as funding was scarce after 1906, he decided to dedicate himself above all to the geometric definition of the architectural forms, in drawings and models, from 1914 onwards. He also abandoned all other work to devote himself totally to the church site. After his death, on 10 June 1926, direction of the site was taken over by his assistant, Domènech Sugranyes i Gras, who by 1930 had completed the top of the bell towers and many of the sculptures, including the large cypress with the alabaster doves on the façade of Birth.

When Sugranyes himself, the last person who had direct knowledge of Gaudí's intentions and wishes, died in 1938, the site was entrusted to Francesc Quintana, who rebuilt the crypt, started restoring the plaster models and built a wall with a large neo-Gothic window in the eastern wing of the transept.

Model of the central nave

In 1954, the Junta Constructora del Temple decided to begin construction of the Passion façade. Fund-raising activities were organized so that the work could continue; this was led initially by Francesc Quintana, then by Isidre Puig i Boada and finally by Lluís Bonet i Garí. By 1976 the architecture of the entire façade, including the four bell towers, was complete. When Quintana died in 1967, the work continued under the direction of Puig Boada and Bonet i Garí until they handed over to Francesc Cardoner i Blanch when they were in their eighties.

In the meantime Jordi Bonet i Armengol became the head architect and took over the supervision of the site. He immediately turned his attention to strengthening the church foundations, building the walls of the aisles and erecting the branch-like columns. Using reinforced concrete and stone formwork that retains the shapes of Gaudí's design, Bonet and his assistants managed to erect the pillars and vaults of the side aisles along the longitudinal axis by 2000, after having consolidated the terrain with dense piling. After 1995, Bonet started studying the realization of the vaults of the

Sagrada Família building site in the early years of construction work, when the surrounding area had not yet been urbanized, 1915

central nave, which he decided to build, using specially trained workers, by the traditional Catalan method of leaves of overlapping tile.

In 1986 the sculptor Josep Maria Subirachs accepted the commission to produce the sculptural cycle on the façade of the Passion; he worked on it for about 15 years, carving around a hundred different figures.

Drawing of the stellar piazza, outlined by Gaudí in November 1916, showing the minimum distance required to gain a good view of the temple

Facing page:
Rear-façade of the Birth

Life and Work

Gaudí smoking a cigar with his father Francesc and a friend, Dr. Pere Santaló, during a summer outing to Montserrat in 1897

1852 ▸ (b Reus, province of Barcelona, 25 June). Son of Francesc Gaudí i Serra, a coppersmith from Riudoms, and Antonia Cornet i Bertran. As a boy, Gaudí helped in his father's workshop. Spent much of his childhood resting in the country as a cure for rheumatic pains, becoming an acute observer of nature. Went to school in Reus.

1869 ▸ Moved with his brother Francesc, a medical student, to Barcelona, where he attended schools to prepare for architectural studies. His father sold property in Reus to fund his children's education and came to live with them in Barcelona.

1873 ▸ Began studying architecture at the School of Fine Arts, transformed in 1875 into the Faculty of Architecture of the University of Barcelona.

1875 ▸ Did military service.

1876–1878 ▸ To fund his studies, he worked as a draughtsman with Josep Fontseré, Director of Works at the Parc de la Ciutadella, Barcelona; the architect Francesc de Paula Villar i Lozano; worked at a machine manufacturing plant called Padrós i Borràs; and with the municipal architect Leandre Serrallach i Mas. His mother and doctor brother died in 1876.

1878 ▸ Graduated as an architect on 15 March. In the workshop of the craftsman Eudald Puntí, he designed and personally constructed his own drawing board. Met the glove manufacturer Esteve

Comella, and designed a showcase for him for the Exposition Universelle in Paris. Undertook modest commissions for Count Eusebi Güell i Bacigalupi. His first projects of a certain importance were: public street-lamps; a cast-iron kiosk; a housing and factory unit for the workers' cooperative La Obrera Mataronense. The industrial unit, covered with wooden parabolic arches, is still standing.
Became a member first of the Catalan Association for Scientific Excursions and then of the Catalonia Excursion Centre, visiting all the major sites of Catalan historical significance.
His sister, Rosa, died, leaving a daughter Rosita, who lived throughout her life with her uncle and maternal grandfather.

1880 1882 ▸ Designed an altar for a college in Tarragona and a kiosk in Comillas. In February 1881, he published, in the magazine *La Reinaxensa*, a critical review of the exhibition of industrial arts held in the city.

1882 ▸ Worked in the studio of his former professor, the architect Joan Martorell i Montells.
Designed a hunting lodge (never built) for Eusebi Güell on the Mediterranean coast at El Garraf.

1883 ▸ Began the construction of Casa Vicens, completed in 1888. Opened the Villa El Capricho site at Comillas, where the Director of Works was Cristóbal Cascante.
On 3 November, on the recommendation of Joan Martorell, he was

appointed chief architect of the Sagrada Família, succeeding Francesc de Paula Villar i Lozano, who had commenced the construction work the previous year. Began work on the Pavellons de la Finca Güell in Barcelona, completed in 1887.

1885 ▸ Designed an altar for the private chapel of publisher and bookseller Josep Maria Bocabella, one of the promoters of the Associació Espiritual de Devots de Sant Josep for the construction of the Sagrada Família. In March he drew up the first plan of the church.

1886 ▸ Construction began on Palau Güell, Barcelona, completed in 1890.

1887 ▸ Constructed a building in the area of the Sagrada Família, used as a design studio. Studied the composition of traditional ceramics with the architect Domènech i Montaner.

1888 ▸ Contributed to building work for the Exposición Universal in Barcelona, designing the pavilion of the Compañía Transatlántica in the maritime section and exhibiting his designs in the architecture section. The mayor of the city commissioned him to refashion the decoration and the steps of honour of the Saló de Cent in the municipal building.

1889 ▸ Father Enric d'Ossó i Cervelló, founder of the religious order of Santa Teresa, commissioned Gaudí to complete the partially built Col·legi de les Teresianes in Barcelona.

1889–1893 ▸ Worked on constructing the Palacio Episcopal in Astorga. After the death of his friend, Joan Baptista Grau i Vallespinós, the Bishop of Astorga, he abandoned the project, which was completed by other architects.

1891–1894 ▸ Built the Casa Fernández y Andrés in Léon.

1892 ▸ Went to Malaga and Tangiers with the Marqués de Comillas to study the area where the Marqués wanted to build a major complex for the Franciscan missions in Africa.

1893 ▸ Completed the crypt and walls of the apse of the Sagrada Família. An austere Lent fast seriously threatened his life.

1895 ▸ Declined the project, never realized, to design a cemetery chapel for the Güell family in Monserrat. The Bodegas Güell in El Garraf are attributed to Gaudí's friend, the architect Francesc Berenguer i Mestres. At all events, the plans were signed by Gaudí, so that we assume the two worked together.

1898–1900 ▸ Built Casa Calvet in Barcelona, which won the city administration's prize for Best Building of the Year. Drew up the first plan for the church of the Colònia Güell, a working-class neighbourhood in Santa Coloma de Cervelló, Barcelona.

1899 ▸ Became a member of the Artistic Circle of St Luke and of the Spiritual League of the Virgin of Montserrat.

1900 ▸ Built the first Glorious Mystery with sculptures, intended as part of a cycle of monumental episodes, never realized, situated in a cave in the mountain of Montserrat.
Began the garden city, commissioned by Eusebi Güell, on the Muntanya Pelada on the outskirts of Barcelona, now the Park Güell, left incomplete in 1914.

1900–1905 ▸ Built Villa Bellesguard, Barcelona.

1902 ▸ Built the Finca Miralles Gate, Barcelona.

1903 ▸ Began work for Pere Campins i Barceló to carry out alterations to the cathedral in Palma de Majorca, where he went occasionally. Work was halted in 1914.

1904 ▸ Realized and decorated the first cinema in Barcelona, Sala Mercè; subsequently destroyed, a smaller version was rebuilt in 2002. Began work to remodel the Casa Batlló, completed in 1906.

1906 ▸ Purchased the show-house in the Park Güell, where he lived with his father and his niece, Rosita. The architect Josep Maria Jujol became his assistant.

1906–1910 ▸ Built Casa Milà, known as "La Pedrera", in Barcelona.
Laid out the Jardins Artigas at La Pobla de Lillet.

1907 ▸ Opening of the building site for the crypt of the Colònia Güell. According to the sculptor Joan Matamala, he was commissioned to design a skyscraper in New York's Manhattan area.

1909 ▸ Built the classrooms of the Sagrada Família.

1910 ▸ For health reasons he spent the spring with friends at Vic. Designed two lamp posts in basalt and cast iron for the Plaça Mayor in Vic, to mark the centenary of the philospher Jaime Balmes.
In Paris the Société des Beaux-Arts holds an exhibition at which several works by Gaudí are shown. Gaudí did not even visit it.

1911 ▶ The Paris exhibition moved to Madrid.
Contracted Malta fever. Retreated to Puigcerdà with a doctor friend, where he drew up his will.

1914 ▶ Abandoned all his other projects to devote himself entirely to work on the Sagrada Família.

1922 ▶ A request arrived from Chile to design a church for the city of Rancagua. Gaudí's proposal for the chapel dedicated to the Virgin was rejected.

1924 ▶ Held by the Barcelona police while going to a Mass to commemorate Catalans who had died defending the city in 1714.

1925 ▶ Now alone, he moved into modest accommodation on the site of the Sagrada Família.

1926 ▶ After being knocked down by a tram, Gaudí died from his injuries in a Barcelona hospital on 10 June.

Gaudí during the Corpus Christi procession in Barcelona, 11 June 1924, at the flag ceremony of the Artistic Circle of St Luke

Spain

Astorga:
Palacio Episcopal

León:
Casa Fernández y Andrés

Comillas:
El Capricho

Santa Coloma de Cervelló:
Cripta de la Colònia Güell

Palma de Majorca:
Catedral de Mallorca

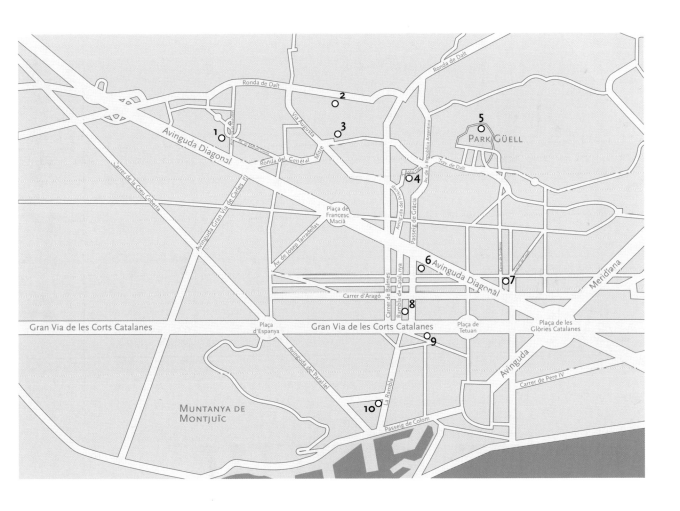

Barcelona

1. **Avinguda de Pedralbes, 7**
Finca Güell

2. **Carrer Bellesguard, 16**
Villa Bellesguard

3. **Carrer Granduxer, 85**
Col·legi de les Teresianes

4. **Carrer de Les Carolines, 18–24**
Casa Vicens

5. **Carrer Olot**
Park Güell

6. **Passeig de Gràcia, 92**
Casa Milà

7. **Plaça de la Sagrada Família**
Sagrada Família / Classrooms

8. **Passeig de Gràcia, 43**
Casa Batlló

9. **Carrer Casp, 48**
Casa Calvet

10. **Carrer Nou de la Rambla, 3–5**
Palau Güell

Bibliography

▶ Antoni Gaudí (1852–1926), Exhibition catalogue, Museum Villa Stuck, Munich 1986, Fundació Caixa de Pensions, Barcelona 1986.
▶ Bassegoda Nonell, Joan und Collins, George R.: The Designs and Drawings of Antonio Gaudí, New Jersey 1983.
▶ Bergós i Massó, Joan (Text) und Llimargas, Marc (Fotografie): Gaudí. The artist and his work, Ostfildern, 2000.
▶ Bonet, Jordi: L'últim Gaudí, Barcelona 2000.
▶ Crippa, Maria Antonietta (text) und Llimargas Casas, Marc (photographs): Gaudí. Interieurs, Furniture, Garden Architecture, Ostfildern 2001.
▶ Crippa, Maria Antonietta und Bassegoda Nonell, Joan (Ed.): Gaudí. Spazio e segni del sacro, Milan 2002.
▶ Flores, Carlos: Gaudí, Jujol y el modernismo catalán, 2 Bde., Aguilar, Madrid 1982.
▶ Giralt-Miracle, Daniel (Ed.): Gaudí 2002. Miscelànea, Barcelona 2002.
▶ Giralt-Miracle, Daniel (Ed.): Gaudí. La búsqueda de la forma. Espacio, geometría, estructura y construcción, Barcelona 2002.
▶ Güell, Xavier: Antoni Gaudí, Zurich and Munich 1987.
▶ Montaner, Josep Maria: Barcelona. City and Architecture, Cologne 1997.
▶ Paris – Barcelona. De Gaudí à Miró, Exhibition catalogue, Galeries Nationales du Grand Palais, Paris, 3.10.2001–14.01.2002, Réunions des Musées Nationaux, Paris 2001.
▶ Permanyer, Lluís (text), Levick, Melba (photographs): Gaudí of Barcelona, New York 1998.
▶ Van Zandt, Eleanor: The life and works of Antoni Gaudí. Parragon Book Service Limited, Bristol 1995.
▶ Zerbst, Rainer: Antoni Gaudí, Taschen, Cologne 2002.

Credits